How I Raised Myself

from

FAILURE TO SUCCESS

In Selling

⇒》 《⇐

How I Raised Myself

from FAILURE

To

SUCCESS IN SELLING

by

Frank Bettger

→》》 《《←

PRENTICE-HALL, INC.

NEW YORK

Second printing, November, 1949
Third printing, February, 1950
Fourth printing, February, 1950
Fifth printing, March, 1950
Sixth printing, April, 1950
Seventh printing, May, 1950
Eighth printing, July, 1950
Ninth printing, February, 1951
Tenth printing, April, 1951
Eleventh printing, August, 1951

To

Hazel, my wife

whose encouragement, guidance and inspiration
are a part of every page in this book.

WHAT I THINK OF THIS BOOK

by Dale Carnegie

->>>   <<<-

I have known the author of this book, Frank Bettger, since 1917. He came up the hard way, got little formal education, never finished grade school. The history of his life is an outstanding American success story.

His father died when he was just a small boy, leaving his mother with five little children. When he was eleven years old, he had to get up at four-thirty in the morning to sell newspapers on street corners to help his widowed mother, who took in washing and sewing in order to help feed her family. Mr. Bettger told me that there were many times when he seldom had anything for his evening meal but corn-meal mush and skimmed milk.

At 14, he had to leave school; took a job as a steamfitter's helper. At eighteen, he became a professional baseball player, and for two years he played third base for the St. Louis Cardinals. Then one day in Chicago, Illinois, while playing against the Chicago Cubs, he injured his arm and was forced to give up baseball.

He drifted back to Philadelphia, his home town—and when

I met him he was 29 years of age, trying to sell life insurance, and was a total failure as a salesman. Yet during the next twelve years, he made enough money to purchase a seventy-thousand-dollar country estate, and could have retired at forty. I know. I saw it happen. I saw him rise from a total failure to one of the most successful and highest paid salesmen in America. In fact, I persuaded him to join me a few years ago and tell his story in a series of one-week schools I was giving under the auspices of the United States Junior Chamber of Commerce, on "Leadership Training, Human Relations and Salesmanship."

Frank Bettger has earned the right to talk and write on this subject, for he has made nearly 40,000 sales calls—the equivalent of five calls every day for more than twenty-five years.

The first chapter, "How One Idea Multiplied My Income and Happiness," is to me the most inspiring address I have ever heard on the power of enthusiasm. Enthusiasm took Frank Bettger out of the ranks of failure and helped transform him into one of the nation's highest-paid salesmen.

I saw Frank Bettger make his first stumbling talk in public, and I have seen him delight and inspire large audiences all the way from Portland, Oregon, to Miami, Florida. After seeing the amazing effect he had on men, I urged him to write a book, relating *his* experiences, *his* techniques, and *his* philosophy of selling, just as he told them to thousands of people throughout the country from the lecture platform.

Here it is—the most helpful and inspiring book on salesmanship I have ever read—a book that will be helping salesmen, regardless of whether they are selling insurance, or shoes, or ships, or sealing-wax, long after Frank Bettger has passed away.

I have read every page of this book. I can recommend it with enthusiasm. Talk about walking a mile to get a cigarette—when I started out to sell, I would gladly have walked from Chicago to New York to get a copy of this book, if it had been available.

HOW I HAPPENED TO WRITE
THIS BOOK

›» «‹

One day, quite by accident, I got on the same train in New York with Dale Carnegie. Dale was bound for Memphis, Tennessee, to deliver some lectures.

He said: "Frank, I have been giving a series of one-week schools, sponsored by the United States Junior Chamber of Commerce; why don't you come along with me and give some talks on selling?"

I thought he was joking. I said: "Dale, you know I didn't finish grade school. I couldn't give lectures on selling."

Dale said: "Just tell them how you raised yourself from failure to success in selling. Just tell them what *you* did."

I thought it over, and I said, "Well, I guess I could do that."

In a short time, Dale and I were delivering lectures all over the country. We talked to the same audience four hours a night for five consecutive nights. Dale would speak for half an hour; then I would talk for half an hour.

Later, Dale said: "Frank, why don't you write a book?

Many of the books on salesmanship are written by people who never did any selling at all. Why don't you write a new kind of book on selling? A book that tells precisely what you did—a book that tells how you raised yourself from a failure to a success in selling. Tell the story of your own life. Put the word 'I' in every sentence. Don't lecture. Just tell the story of your life as a salesman."

The more I thought about this, the more I thought it would sound egotistical.

"I don't want to do that," I said.

But Dale spent one whole afternoon with me, pleading with me to tell my own story, just as I had from the lecture platform.

Dale said: "In every city where we gave our lectures, those Junior Chamber of Commerce boys asked whether Frank Bettger was putting his lectures in the form of a book. You probably thought that young man in Salt Lake City was joking when he put down $40 in advance, for the first copy of it—but he wasn't. He knew it would be worth many times $40 to him. . . ."

So, in a short time, I was writing a book.

In these pages, I have tried to tell the story of my stupid blunders and mistakes, and precisely what I did that lifted me out of the ranks of failure and despair. When I broke into selling, I had two strikes on me. I didn't know any more about selling than a jack-rabbit. My eight years in baseball seemed to unfit me for anything even remotely like selling. If Lloyds of London had been betting on me, they would have bet a thousand to one that I would fail. And

I didn't have much more confidence in myself than Lloyds would have had.

I hope you will overlook and forgive me for using the personal pronoun "I." If there is anything in this book that sounds as though I'm bragging about myself, I didn't intend it that way. Whatever bragging I've done was meant for what these ideas did for me, and what they will do for *anyone* who will apply them.

I have attempted to write the kind of book that I tried to find when I first started to sell. Here it is. I hope you like it.

CONTENTS

→≫≫   ≪≪←

PART FOUR

HOW TO MAKE PEOPLE WANT TO DO BUSINESS WITH YOU

PART FIVE

STEPS IN THE SALE

PART SIX

DON'T BE AFRAID TO FAIL

Part One

THESE IDEAS LIFTED ME OUT OF THE RANKS OF FAILURE

1.
HOW ONE IDEA MULTIPLIED
MY INCOME AND HAPPINESS

❧❧ ❦❦

SHORTLY after I started out as a professional baseball player, I got one of the biggest shocks of my life. That was back in 1907. I was playing for Johnstown, Pennsylvania, in the Tri-State League. I was young and ambitious—wanted to get to the top—and what happened? I was fired! My whole life might have been different if I hadn't gone to the manager and asked him *why* he fired me. In fact, I wouldn't have the rare privilege of writing this book if I hadn't asked him that question.

The manager said he fired me because I was lazy! Well, that was the last thing I expected him to say.

"You drag yourself around the field like a veteran who has been playing ball for twenty years," he told me. "Why do you act that way if you're not lazy?"

"Well, Bert," I said, "I'm so nervous, so scared, that I want to hide my fear from the crowd, and especially from the other players on the team. Besides, I hope that by taking it easy, I'll get rid of my nervousness."

"Frank," he said, "it will never work. That's the thing that is holding you down. Whatever you do after you leave here, for heaven's sake, wake yourself up, and put some life and enthusiasm into your work!"

I had been making $175 a month at Johnstown. After being fired there, I went down to Chester, Pennsylvania, in the Atlantic League, where they paid me only $25 a month. Well, I couldn't feel very enthusiastic on that kind of money, but I began to *act* enthusiastic. After I was there three days, an old ball player, Danny Meehan, came to me and said: "Frank, what in the world are you doing down here in a rank bush-league like this?"

"Well, Danny," I replied, "if I knew how to get a better job, I'd go anywhere."

A week later, Danny induced New Haven, Connecticut, to give me a trial. My first day in New Haven will always stand out in my memory as a great event in my life. No one knew me in that league, so I made a resolution that nobody would ever accuse me of being lazy. I made up my mind to establish the reputation of being the most enthusiastic ball player they'd ever seen in the New England League. I thought if I could establish such a reputation, then I'd have to live up to it.

From the minute I appeared on the field, I acted like a man electrified. I acted as though I were alive with a million batteries. I threw the ball around the diamond so fast and so hard that it almost knocked our infielders' hands apart. Once, apparently trapped, I slid into third base with so much energy and force that the third baseman fumbled the ball and I was able to score an important run. Yes, it was all a show, an act I was putting on. The thermometer

that day was nearly 100°. I wouldn't have been surprised
if I had dropped over with a sunstroke the way I ran around
the field.

Did it work? It worked like magic. Three things happened:

1. My enthusiasm almost entirely overcame my
fear. In fact my nervousness began to work *for* me,
and I played far better than I ever thought I was
capable of playing. (If you are nervous be thankful. Don't hold it back. Turn it on. Let your
nerves work *for* you.)

2. My enthusiasm affected the other players on
the team, and they too became enthusiastic.

3. Instead of dropping with the heat, I felt better
during the game and after it was over than I had
ever felt before.

My biggest thrill came the following morning when I read
in the New Haven newspaper: "This new player, Bettger,
has a barrel of enthusiasm. He inspired our boys. They
not only won the game, but looked better than at any time
this season."

The newspapers began calling me "Pep" Bettger—the life
of the team. I mailed the newspaper clippings to Bert Conn,
manager of Johnstown. Can you imagine the expression on
his face as he read about "Pep" Bettger, the dub he'd tied a
can to three weeks before—for being *lazy?*

Within ten days, *enthusiasm* took me from $25 a month
to $185 a month—it increased my income by 700 per cent.
Let me repeat—nothing but the determination to act en-

thusiastic increased my income 700 per cent in ten days! I got this stupendous increase in salary not because I could throw a ball better—or catch or hit better, not because I had any more ability as a ball player. I didn't know any more about baseball than I did before.

Two years later—two years from the time I had been hoping to get $25 a month in that little Chester outfit, I was playing third base for the St. Louis Cardinals and had multiplied my income by thirty times. What did it? Enthusiasm alone did it; nothing but enthusiasm.

Two years after that, while playing a game in Chicago against the Chicago Cubs, I had a bad accident. Picking up a swinging bunt while on a full run, I attempted to throw in the opposite direction. Something snapped in my arm. That accident forced me to give up baseball. This seemed like a great tragedy to me at the time, but I now look back on it as one of the most fortunate events of my life.

I returned home, and for the next two years made my living riding around the streets of Philadelphia on a bicycle. I was a collector for an installment furniture concern; one dollar down and the balance in "uneasy" weekly payments. After two dismal years of collecting installments, I decided to try selling insurance with the Fidelity Mutual Life Insurance Company.

The next ten months were the longest and most disheartening months of my life.

A dismal failure at selling life insurance, I finally concluded that *I was never cut out to be a salesman,* and began answering want ads for a job as a shipping clerk. I realized, however, that no matter what work I tried to do, I had to overcome a strange fear-complex that possessed me, so I joined one of Dale Carnegie's courses in public speaking. One night, Mr. Carnegie stopped me in the middle of a talk.

"Mr. Bettger," he said. "Just a moment . . . just a moment. Are you interested in what you are saying?"

"Yes . . . of course I am," I replied.

"Well, then," said Mr. Carnegie, "why don't you talk with a little enthusiasm? How do you expect your audience to be interested if you don't put some life and animation into what you say?"

Dale Carnegie then gave our class a stirring talk on the power of enthusiasm. He got so excited during his talk, he threw a chair up against the wall and broke off one of its legs.

Before I went to bed that night, I sat for an hour thinking. My thoughts went back to my baseball days at Johnstown and New Haven. For the first time, I realized that the very fault which had threatened to wreck my career in baseball was now threatening to wreck my career as a salesman.

The decision I made that night was the turning point of my life. That decision was to stay in the insurance business and put the same enthusiasm into selling that I had put into playing baseball when I joined the New Haven team.

I shall never forget the first call I made the next day. It was my first "crashing through" session. I made up my mind that I was going to show my prospect the most enthusiastic salesman he'd ever seen in his life. As I pounded my fist with excitement, I expected every minute to have the man stop me and ask if there was anything wrong with me, but he didn't.

At one stage of the interview, I noticed he raised himself to a more erect position and opened his eyes wider, but he never stopped me, except to ask questions. Did he throw me out? No, he bought! This man, Al Emmons, a grain merchant in the Bourse Building, Philadelphia, soon became one of my good friends and best boosters.

From that day on, I began to sell. The Magic of Enthusiasm began to work for me in business, just as it had in baseball.

I would not want to give anybody the impression that I think enthusiasm consists of fist-pounding . . . but if fist-pounding is what you need to arouse yourself inside, then I am overwhelmingly for it. I know this: When I force myself to *act* enthusiastic, I soon *feel* enthusiastic.

During my thirty-two years of selling, I have seen enthusiasm double and treble the income of dozens of salesmen, and I have seen the lack of it cause hundreds of salesmen to fail.

I firmly believe enthusiasm is by far the biggest single factor in successful selling. For example, I know a man who is an authority on insurance—he could even write a book on the subject—and yet he can't make a decent living selling it. Why? Largely because of his lack of enthusiasm.

I know another salesman who didn't know one-tenth as much about insurance, yet he made a fortune selling it, and retired in twenty years. His name is Stanley Gettis. He now lives in Miami Beach, Florida. The reason for his outstanding success was not knowledge—it was enthusiasm.

Can you acquire enthusiasm—or must you be born with it? Certainly you can acquire it! Stanley Gettis acquired it. He became a human dynamo. How? Just by forcing himself each day to *act* enthusiastic. As a part of his plan, Stanley Gettis repeated a poem almost every morning for twenty years. He found that repeating it helped him generate enthusiasm for the day. I found this poem so inspiring that I had it printed on a card and gave away hundreds of them. It was written by Herbert Kauffman and has a good title . . .

VICTORY

You are the man who used to boast
That you'd achieve the uttermost,
Some day.

You merely wished a show,
To demonstrate how much you know
And prove the distance you can go. . . .

Another year we've just passed through.
What new ideas came to you?
How many big things did you do?

Time . . . left twelve fresh months in your care
How many of them did you share
With opportunity and dare
Again where you so often missed?

We do not find you on the list of Makers Good.
Explain the fact!
Ah no, 'twas not the chance you lacked!
As usual—you failed to act!

Why don't you memorize this poem, and repeat it daily. It may do for you what it did for Stanley Gettis.

Once I read a statement made by Walter P. Chrysler. I was so impressed by it, I carried it in my pocket for a week. I'll bet I read it over forty times, until I knew it by heart. I wish every salesman would memorize it. Walter Chrysler, when asked to give the secret of success, listed the various qualities, such as ability, capacity, energy, but added that the real secret was enthusiasm. "Yes, more than enthusiasm," said Chrysler, "I would say excitement. I like to see men get excited. When they get excited, they get customers excited, and we get business."

Enthusiasm is by far the highest paid quality on earth, probably because it is one of the rarest; yet it is one of the most contagious. If you are enthusiastic, your listener is very likely to become enthusiastic, even though you may present your ideas poorly. Without enthusiasm, your sales talk is about as dead as last year's turkey.

Enthusiasm isn't merely an outward expression. Once you begin to acquire it, enthusiasm works constantly within you. You may be sitting quietly in your home . . . an idea occurs to you . . . that idea begins to develop . . . finally, you become consumed with enthusiasm . . . nothing can stop you.

It will help you overcome fear, become more successful

in business, make more money, enjoy a healthier, richer and happier life.

When can you begin? Right now. Just say to yourself, "This is one thing I can do."

How can you begin? There is just one rule:

To become enthusiastic—act enthusiastic.

Put this rule into action for thirty days and be prepared to see astonishing results. It may easily revolutionize your entire life.

Stand up on your hind legs each morning, and repeat with powerful gestures and all the enthusiasm you can generate, these words:

Force yourself to act enthusiastic, and you'll become enthusiastic!

I urge you to reread many times this chapter by Frank Bettger, and to make a high and holy resolve that you will double the amount of enthusiasm that you have been putting into your work and into your life. If you carry out that resolve, you will probably double your income and double your happiness.

DALE CARNEGIE

2. ♦ THIS IDEA PUT ME BACK INTO SELLING AFTER I HAD QUIT

→≫≫   ≪←

LOOKING back across the years, I am astounded how trivialities have changed the entire course of my life. As I have already said, after ten miserable, disheartening months trying to sell life insurance, I gave up all hope of ever being able to sell anything. I resigned, and I spent several days answering want-ads. I wanted a job as a shipping clerk, because as a boy I had worked for the American Radiator Company, hammering nails into crates and stenciling them for shipment. With my limited education, I thought I could qualify for that kind of work. But try as I did, I couldn't even get a job as a shipping clerk.

I was not only discouraged; I was in the depths of despair. I figured that I'd have to go back to riding my bicycle and collecting installments for George Kelly's. My highest hope was to get my old job back at $18 a week.

I had left a fountain pen, and penknife—and a few other personal things at the insurance company office. So one morning I went back to get them. I expected to be there only a few minutes, but while I was cleaning out my desk, the president of the company, Mr. Walter LeMar Talbot, and all of the salesmen came into the "bull pen" to hold a meeting. I couldn't leave without embarrassment, so I sat there and listened to several salesmen make talks. The more they talked, the more discouraged I got. They were talking about things I knew I couldn't possibly do. Then I heard the president, Mr. Talbot, utter one sentence that has had a profound and lasting effect on my life for the past thirty-one years. *That sentence was this:*

Gentlemen, after all, this business of selling narrows down to one thing—just one thing . . . seeing the people! Show me any man of ordinary ability who will go out and earnestly tell his story to four or five people every day, and I will show you a man who just can't help making good!

Well, that lifted me right out of my chair. I'd believe anything that Mr. Talbot said. Here was a man who had started working for the company when he was eleven years old; worked his way through every department; had actually been out on the street selling for several years. He knew what he was talking about. It was just as though the sun had suddenly burst out from the clouds. I made up my mind right then to take him at his word.

I said to myself, "Look here, Frank Bettger, you've got two good legs. You can go out and earnestly tell your story to four or five people every day; so you are going to make good—Mr. Talbot said so!"

My but I was happy. What a great relief came over me, —for I knew I was going to make good!

That was just ten weeks before the end of the year. I decided during that time to keep a record of the number of calls I made, just to be sure that I did see at least four people every day. By keeping these records, I discovered that I could make a great many more calls. But I also discovered that to average seeing four people every day, week after week, was a big job. It made me realize how few people I really had been seeing previously.

During those ten weeks, I sold $51,000 of life insurance—more than I had been able to sell during the entire previous ten months! It wasn't much, but it proved to me that Mr. Talbot knew what he was talking about. I could sell!

Then I became aware that my time was worth something, and I determined in the future to waste as little of it as possible. I didn't think it was necessary, however, to continue keeping records.

From then on, for some reason, my sales fell off. A few months later, I found myself back in as big a rut as I had been before. One Saturday afternoon, I took myself back to the office, locked myself in a little conference room, and sat down. For three hours, I sat there having it out with myself: "What's the matter with me? Just what *is* wrong?"

There was only one conclusion. I finally narrowed it down to one thing. I had to admit it. I wasn't seeing the people.

"How am I going to *make* myself see the people?" I thought. "I certainly have incentive enough. I need the money. I'm *not* lazy."

Finally, I determined to go back to keeping records.

One year later, I proudly stood up before our agency and enthusiastically told my story. *I had secretly kept complete records of my calls for twelve months.* They were accurate, for the figures were put down every day. I had made 1,849 calls. Out of these calls, I had interviewed 828 people, closed 65 sales, and my commission amounted to $4,251.82.

How much was each call worth? I figured it out. Each call I had made netted me $2.30. Think of it! One year previously, I had been so discouraged that I resigned. Now, every call I made, *regardless of whether I saw the man or not, put $2.30 down in my pocket.*

I never could find words to express the courage and faith these records gave me.

Later on, I will show how keeping records helped me organize myself so that I was gradually able to increase the value of my *calls* from $2.30 to $19.00 each; how over a period of years, I cut down my average of closing only 1 out of 29 to 1 out of 25, then 1 out of 20, 1 out of 10, and finally 1 out of 3. Let me give just one example now:

The records showed that 70 per cent of my sales were made on the first interview, 23 per cent on the second, and 7 per cent on the third and after. But listen to this: 50 per cent of my time was spent going after the 7 per cent. "So why bother with the 7 per cent," I thought. "Why not put all of my time on first and second interviews?" That decision alone increased the value of each call from $2.80 to $4.27.

Without records, we have no way of knowing what we are doing wrong. I can get more inspiration out of studying my own records, than anything I can read in a magazine. Clay W. Hamlin, one of the world's greatest salesmen, has often inspired me as he has thousands of others. Clay told me he failed three times in selling before he began keeping records.

"You can't hit 'em if you don't swing at 'em," I found was just as true in selling as in baseball. When I played with the Cardinals, we had a right-fielder named Steve Evans. Steve was a big, powerful fellow, built on the lines of Babe Ruth, and he could hit a ball almost as hard as the Babe. But Steve had a bad habit. The habit of waiting. He usually had two strikes called on him before he began swinging. I remember one important game in St. Louis—it was Steve's turn to bat in the ninth inning with two out and the bases full. Any kind of a hit would have won the game. Steve picked out his favorite bat and started for the plate. Everybody yelled: "Come on, Steve, hit that first ball!"

Taking his position at the plate, you could see Steve intended to slam that first one . . . the ball shot straight across the heart of the plate . . . but Evans never moved the bat off his shoulder.

"S-trike one," roared the umpire.

"Come on, Steve! Swing at that next ball!" pleaded the players and the crowd.

Steve dug his spikes deep in the ground for a fresh toehold. Again the pitcher delivered one right through the middle!

Again, Steve failed to swing. "St-rike t-w-o!" bellowed the ump.

"Evans!" screamed Roger Bresnahan, our manager, from the third-base coaching line. "What the hell yuh waitin' for?"

"The first and fifteenth, watta yuh think!" Steve yelled back in disgust. (The 1st and 15th were paydays.)

Every time I see salesmen sitting around the office during selling hours, playing solitaire with prospect cards, I again see Steve Evans up there with his bat on his shoulder, letting the good ones go by—and I hear Bresnahan yell: "Evans, what the hell yuh waitin' for?"

Selling is the easiest job in the world if you work it hard— but the *hardest* job in the world if you try to work it easy.

You know, a good doctor doesn't treat the effects. He treats the *cause*. So let's get right down to the bottom of this proposition of selling:

> You can't collect your commission until you make the sale;
> You can't make the sale, 'til you write the order;
> You can't write the order, 'til you have an interview;
> And you can't have an interview 'til you make the *call!*

There is the whole thing in a nutshell. There is the whole foundation of this business of selling—Calls!

3. ONE THING I DID THAT HELPED ME DESTROY THE BIGGEST ◆ ENEMY I EVER HAD TO FACE

⊢≫≫   ≪≪⊣

MY EARNINGS were so small during that first year, I took a part time job coaching the Swarthmore College baseball team.

One day, I received an invitation from the Y.M.C.A. of Chester, Pa., to come down there and speak on "The Three C's: Clean Living; Clean Character; and Clean Sport." As I read that letter, I realized how utterly impossible it would be for me to accept their invitation. In fact, it suddenly dawned on me that I didn't have the courage to talk convincingly to even one man, let alone one hundred.

It was then I began to realize that before I could ever hope to make good in anything, I would have to overcome this timidity and fear of talking to strangers.

The next day, I went around to the Y.M.C.A., 1421 Arch Street, Philadelphia, and told the educational director why I thought I was a failure. I asked if they had any course that would help me. He smiled, and said: "We have exactly what you need. Come on back with me."

I followed him down a long hallway. We entered a room where a group of men were seated. One man had just finished speaking, and another man was up on his feet criticizing the speaker. We sat down in the back of the room. The educational director whispered to me: "This is a public speaking course."

I had never heard of a "public speaking course."

Just then, another man got up and began to make a speech. He was terrible. In fact, he was so terrible, he encouraged me. I said to myself, "Scared and dumb as I am, I couldn't be much worse than that."

Pretty soon the man who had been criticizing the previous speaker came back. I was introduced to him. His name was *Dale Carnegie*.

I said, "I want to join." He said, "Our course is about half way through. Perhaps you would rather wait. We'll be starting another class in January."

"No," I said, "I want to join right now."

"All right," Mr. Carnegie smiled, and said as he took my arm: "You're the next speaker."

Of course, I was trembling—in fact I was *terrified*—but somehow I managed to tell them why I was there. It was pretty terrible, but terrible as my talk was, it was a tremendous victory for me. Prior to that, I couldn't even stand in front of a crowd and say "How do you do."

This happened thirty years ago to the month I am writing these lines, but that night will always stand out in my memory as the beginning of what proved to be one of the most important phases in my life.

I enrolled for this training then and there, and attended the weekly meetings regularly.

Two months later I went down to Chester and made that speech. I had already learned that it was comparatively easy to talk about my own experiences, so I told the audience at Chester about my experiences in baseball, about my rooming with Miller Huggins, and about how I broke into the big leagues with Christy Mathewson pitching. I was astounded at the fact that I could keep going for almost half an hour, and I was even more astounded, when twenty or thirty men came up afterward, shook my hand, and told me how much they enjoyed it.

That was one of the biggest triumphs in my life. It gave me confidence as nothing else had ever done before. It all seemed like a miracle to me. It *was* a miracle. Two months previously, I was afraid to talk to anyone in an official capacity—now, here I was, standing before a group of 100 people and holding their attention, and enjoying the experience. I went out of that room a changed man.

I had made myself better known in that group by one twenty-five-minute speech than I could have done by attending for months as a silent member.

To my surprise, J. Borton Weeks, prominent Delaware County attorney, who had acted as chairman of the meeting, walked down to the station with me. As I stepped on the train, he shook my hand, thanked me profusely, and invited me to come down again the first chance I could find. "One of my law partners and I have been talking about buying some life insurance," he said, as the train began to move.

I "found the chance" to go back to Chester surprisingly soon.

A few years after that, J. Borton Weeks became president of the Keystone Automobile Club, second largest automobile club in the world. Borton Weeks became one of my best personal friends and, in addition, one of my best centers of influence in business.

As profitable as this connection became, it was nothing compared to the self-confidence and courage I gained through the training I got in taking this course in public speaking. It broadened my vision, and stimulated my enthusiasm; it helped me to express my ideas more convincingly to other men; and it helped me destroy the biggest enemy I ever had to face—*fear*.

I would urge any man or woman who is being held back by fear, and who lacks courage and self-confidence, to join the best public-speaking course in his or her community. Don't join just *any* lecture course. Join only a course where you make a talk at every meeting because that's what you want—experience in speaking.

If you can't find a good, practical course, do as Ben Franklin did. Ben recognized the great value of such training, and he formed the "Junto" right here in my home town. Meet one night each week. Appoint a new chairman to serve each week or month. If you can't get a good instructor, criticize each other, as the Junto did 200 years ago.

I noticed that the members of our class who got the most benefit out of it and showed the biggest improvement were those who put their training to some practical use. So, as poor as I was, I sought opportunities to speak in public. I nearly died of stage-fright at first, but I did it somehow.

I even taught a Sunday school class of eight boys. Later, I accepted the superintendency of the Sunday school. I continued to be superintendent for nine years. The effect of this training and experience carried over into my private conversations with individuals. This was one of the finest experiences I have ever had.

All the leaders and successful men I've ever met have had courage and self-confidence, and most of them, I notice, are able to express themselves convincingly.

The best way I ever found to help overcome fear and develop courage and self-confidence rapidly is by speaking before groups. I discovered that when I lost my fear of speaking to audiences, I lost my fear of talking to individuals, no matter how big and important they were. This training and experience in public speaking got me out of my shell, opened my eyes to my own possibilities, and widened my horizons. It was one of the turning points in my career.

4. THE ONLY WAY I COULD GET MYSELF ORGANIZED

⇥≫   ≪↤

NOT LONG after I began keeping records, I discovered that I was one of the world's poorest self-organizers. I had set a goal of 2,000 calls for the year, at the rate of forty a week. But I soon got so hopelessly behind that I was ashamed to put down any records. My intentions were good. I kept making new resolutions but they never lasted very long. I just *couldn't* get organized.

Finally I got it through my head that I must take more time for planning. It was easy to throw forty or fifty prospect cards together and think I was prepared. *That* didn't take much time. But to go back over records, study each call carefully, plan exactly what I would say to each person, prepare proposals, write letters, and then make out a schedule, arranging each day's calls, Monday through Friday, in their proper order, required four to five solid hours of the most intensive kind of work.

So I set aside Saturday morning, and called it "self-organization day." Did this plan help me? Listen! Each Monday morning, when I started out, instead of having to drive myself to make calls, I walked in to see men with confidence and enthusiasm. I was eager and *anxious* to see them, because I had thought about them, studied their situation, and had some ideas I believed might be of value to them. At the end of the week, instead of feeling exhausted and discouraged, I actually felt exhilarated and on fire with the excitement that next week I could do even better.

After a few years, I was able to move my "self-organization day" up to Friday morning, then knock off the rest of the week, forgetting business entirely until Monday morning. It is surprising how much I can get done when I take enough time for planning, and it is perfectly amazing how little I get done without it. I prefer to work on a tight schedule four and a half days a week and get somewhere than to be working all the time and never get anywhere.

I read that Henry L. Doherty, the great industrialist, said: "I can hire men to do everything but two things, *think,* and *do things in the order of their importance.*"

That was my trouble precisely. However, after solving that problem each week for so many years, I believe the real answer is simply this: Take enough time to think and plan.

At the close of this chapter, you will see a typical "weekly timetable." I didn't just make it up as a sample. I pulled a few out of my files and used one of them for illustration. You will also see one month's exhibit of "record cards," which may also be helpful to anyone planning his time.

Yes, I can hear you say, "That's not for me! I can't do that sort of thing—live on a schedule. I wouldn't be happy." Well, I've got good news for you. *You are already living on a schedule.* And, if it's not a planned one, it's probably a poor one. Let me give you an example: Several years ago, a young man came to me for advice. He had graduated with high honors from one of our oldest and finest colleges, and had gone into selling with a lot of promise. Now, after two years, he was badly discouraged. He said, "Mr. Bettger, tell me frankly, do you think I am cut out to be a salesman?"

"No, Ed," I replied, "I don't think you are cut out to be a a salesman."

His face dropped, but I continued. "I don't think *anybody* is cut out to be a salesman—or anything else. *I think we've got to cut ourselves out to be whatever we want to be.*"

"I don't understand," said Ed. "I always seem to be busy and working. Why, I don't have time to go buy myself a necktie. If I could just get organized!"

Now I happened to know that this young fellow was a late starter. So I said, "Ed, why don't you join the 'Six o'Clock Club'?"

"The 'Six o'Clock Club'?" he asked. "What's that?"

"A number of years ago," I explained, "I read that Ben Franklin said that only a few men live to old age, and fewer still ever become successful who are not early risers. So I set my alarm clock an hour and a half earlier in the morning. An hour of that time I used for reading and study. Of course, I soon found myself going to bed earlier, but I thrived on it."

That day Ed agreed to buy an alarm clock and join the

"Six o'Clock Club." He set aside Saturday morning for "self-organization day." Soon his troubles were behind him, and Ed was selling successfully. Only four years later, he was appointed manager of a large eastern territory by one of the great industrial companies.

Not long ago I interviewed one of the executives of the International Business Machines Corporation, a company which holds one of the highest ratings in the world for sales-training methods. I asked him how important they consider their "Weekly Work Sheet."

He said: "Mr. Bettger, we furnish our salesmen with certain tools which we know are essential to their success. Our number one tool is the "Weekly Work Sheet," which must be completed by the salesmen, giving the names of all the people they plan to see during the coming week, and a copy must be turned over to us in *advance* of each week's work."

"Do you enforce this rule in all of the seventy-nine countries in which you operate?" I asked.

"Absolutely," he replied.

"What would happen," I asked, "if a salesman refused to use this number one tool?"

"It couldn't happen. But if it did, the salesman couldn't work for us."

Those were his exact words.

Most of the successful men I've met are absolutely ruthless with their time. For example, Lawrence Doolin, one of the officials of the Fidelity Mutual Life Insurance Company of Philadelphia, told me the other day about an experience he had recently. Larry called their Altoona, Pennsylvania, manager, Richard W. Campbell, on the telephone one night and said: "Dick, I'm starting on a western trip next week to visit several of our agencies. Monday I'll be in Harrisburg. Tuesday, I'd like to spend in Altoona with you."

Dick replied, "Larry, I'm anxious to see you, but it would be impossible for me to see you before next Friday afternoon."

The following Friday, as the two men sat down together at lunch, Larry began: "Were you away all week, Dick?"

"No," answered Dick, "I've been around all week."

Surprised, Larry said, "Do you mean to say you were here in Altoona on Tuesday?"

"Yes," smiled Dick.

With considerable feeling of resentment, Larry said: "Dick, do you realize what you made me do? You made me retrack my steps all the way from Cincinnati! Tonight I must go back again, and from there to Detroit."

Dick Campbell then explained: "Listen, Larry, before you phoned me, I had spent five hours last Friday morning planning this entire week. Tuesday was one of the biggest days. Several appointments had already been arranged. To have spent Tuesday with you, would have interrupted my whole week's schedule. Please don't feel offended, Larry. If it had been E. A. Roberts, the president of the company, I'd have done the same thing. Whatever success I've had in this business has been due to the fact that I refuse to allow anything or anybody to interfere with the schedule of the week which I devote every Friday to preparing."

Larry Doolin said to me: "Frank, when I first heard this

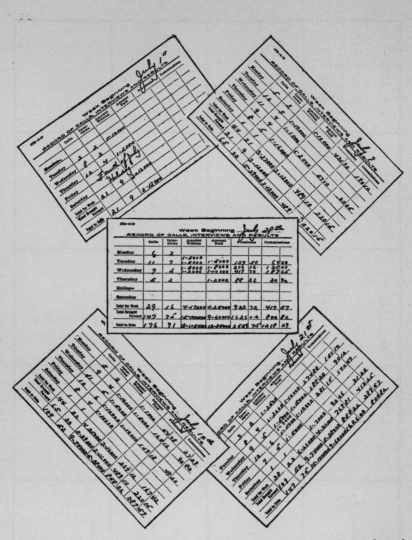

Exhibit of one month's record cards, showing actual results of
planning, and commissions earned.

WEEKLY TIME TABLE

	Mon. 6/14	Tues. 6/15	Wed. 6/16	Thur. 6/17	Fri. 6/18
MORNING	Rosengarten Siano	Buehler Boryer Dick	Coale Felton McClennen	Madden Hazlett Weaver	Haircut 8 A.M. Planning 8:45 to 1
LUNCH	Quigley	Trout	McBride	Kroll	
AFTERNOON	Connelly Dutcher Dick	Lueders Ackley Rigley Levick	Silver Horst Karl	Fretz Paoli Stiefel Derry	
EVENING	Paul Fisher		Henze		

Typical "weekly timetable," which helped me get organized.

I was shocked. But I didn't let myself get angry. I quickly realized that here was the *real secret* of Dick Campbell's phenomenal rise to success."

Larry told me that when he got on the train that night he was fired with a new enthusiasm. Since that time he has been telling this story to salesmen all over the country.

Back in 1926 I spent most of the summer on Eaton's Dude Ranch, located in the foothills of the Big Horn Mountains, near Sheridan, Wyoming. Mary Roberts Rinehart, author of more than fifty novels and one of the highest paid writers in America, made her summer home there. I asked Mrs. Rinehart how she happened to become a writer. Here are her own words:

> I always thought I could learn to write, if I just had the time, but I had three small sons, and my husband to look after . . . also my mother, who for several years was a helpless invalid. Then, during a financial panic, we lost everything. I was driven frantic by debts. I made up my mind I was going to earn some money by writing, so I made up a schedule, planning every hour for the week in advance. Certain periods during the day and in the evening after I got the children off to bed while Dr. Rinehart was out making calls, I set aside for writing.

I asked Mrs. Rinehart if working on such a tight schedule didn't wear her down. "On the contrary," she smiled, "my life took on a new zest."

Mary Roberts Rinehart didn't know how much she inspired me.   After I returned home, I did a far better job than I had ever done before of managing Frank Bettger and his time.

I ran across a poem years ago by Douglas Malloch.   I cut it out and put it in my scrapbook.   I read it and reread it until I knew it by heart.   It did something for me.   Maybe it will do something for you.   Here it is: *

There may be nothing wrong with you,
The way you live, the work you do,
But I can very plainly see
Exactly what is wrong with me.
It isn't that I'm indolent
Or dodging duty by intent;
I work as hard as anyone,
And yet I get so little done,
The morning goes, the noon is here,
Before I know, the night is near,
And all around me, I regret,
Are things I haven't finished yet.
If I could just get organized!
I oftentimes have realized
Not all that matters is the *man;*
The man must also have a plan.

＊   ＊   ＊

With you, there may be nothing wrong,
But here's my trouble right along;
I do the things that don't amount
To very much, of no account,

* Reprinted by permission of Mrs. Douglas Malloch.

That really seem important though
And let a lot of matters go.
I nibble this, I nibble that,
But never finish what I'm at.
I work as hard as anyone,
And yet, I get so little done,
I'd do so much you'd be surprised,
If I could just get organized!

SUMMARY

PART ONE

POCKET REMINDERS

1. Force yourself to *act* enthusiastic, and you'll *become* enthusiastic. "Make a high and holy resolve that you will double the amount of enthusiasm that you have been putting into your work and into your life. If you carry out that resolve, you will probably double your income, and double your happiness."

    How can you begin? There is just one rule: "To become enthusiastic, *act* enthusiastic!"

2. Remember the one sentence uttered by Walter LeMar Talbot. "After all, this business of selling narrows down to one thing, just one thing, seeing the people. Show me any man of ordinary ability who will go out and earnestly tell his story to four or five people every day, and I will show you a man who *just can't help making good!*"

3. If you want to overcome fear and develop courage and self-confidence rapidly, join a good course in public speaking. Not just a lecture course. Join only a course where you make a talk at every meeting. When you lose your fear of speaking to an audience, you lose your fear of talking to individuals, no matter how big and important they are.

4. One of the greatest satisfactions in life comes from getting things done and knowing you have done them to the best of your ability. If you are having trouble getting yourself organized, if you want to increase your ability to think, and do things in the order of their importance, remember there is only one way: *Take more time* to think and do things in the order of their importance. Set aside one day as Self-organization day, or a definite period each week. The whole secret of freedom from anxiety over not having enough time lies not in working more hours, but in the proper *planning* of hours.

Part Two

FORMULA FOR SUCCESS
IN SELLING

⋙ ⋘

5. HOW I LEARNED THE MOST IMPORTANT SECRET OF ◆ SALESMANSHIP

▶▶▶ ◀◀◀

ONE WARM August morning I walked into the offices of John Scott and Company, large wholesale grocers, American and Diamond Streets, Philadelphia, and asked for Mr. John Scott. One of his sons, Harry said, "Dad's very busy this morning. Was he expecting you?"

"I don't have an appointment with him," I replied, "but he requested some information from my company, and I've called to give it to him."

"Well," said the son, "you've struck the wrong day. Dad's got three men in his office now, and—"

Just then John Scott walked through and started out into the warehouse.

"Dad!" called the son, "here's a man who wants to see you."

"Did you want to see me, young man?" spoke the boss, glancing back at me as he hurried on through the swinging door into the warehouse.

I followed him, and here is the standing-up interview that followed:

ME. Mr. Scott, my name is Bettger. You requested some

information from us, and I've called to give it to you *(handing him the card he'd signed and returned by mail to my company)*.

SCOTT *(looking at card)*. Well, young man, I don't want the information, but I thought I might as well get the memorandum book your company said they had set aside for me. They wrote me several letters saying they had a book with my name on it, so I sent in the card for it.

ME *(handing him the memo book)*. Mr. Scott, these little booklets never sell any life insurance for us, but they do get us in, and give us an opportunity to tell our story.

SCOTT. Well, there are three men in my office, and I'll be tied up for quite a while. Besides it would be a waste of time to discuss insurance. I'm 63 years old; stopped buying insurance years ago. Most of my policies are paid up. My children are all grown and better able to take care of themselves than I am. There is only my wife and one daughter left with me now, and if anything happened to me, they would have more money than is good for them.

ME. Mr. Scott, a man who has been as successful in life as you have surely must have some interests outside of your family and your business. Perhaps a hospital, religious work, missionary or charitable work of some worthy purpose. Did you ever consider that when you die your support will be withdrawn? Wouldn't this loss seriously handicap or even mean the discontinuance of some splendid work?

(He didn't answer my question, but I could tell by the expression on his face that I'd struck oil. He waited for me to go on.)

Through our plan, Mr. Scott, you can absolutely guarantee them your support—live or die. If you live, seven years from now you will begin to receive an income of $5,000 a year in monthly checks as long as you live. If you don't need this income, you can give it away, but if you ever *should* need it, it would be a great blessing to you!

SCOTT *(looking at his watch)*. If you want to wait a little while, I'd like to ask you some questions about this.

ME. I'll be glad to wait.

(About twenty minutes later, I was told to go into Mr. Scott's private office.)

SCOTT. Now what is your name?

ME. Bettger.

SCOTT. Mr. Bettger, you spoke of charities. I support three foreign missionaries, and I *do* give away considerable money each year to things that are very close to my heart. Now just how did you mean this plan would guarantee them my support if I should die? Then you say seven years from now I would begin receiving an income of $5,000 a year—how much would that cost me?

(When I told him the cost, he looked startled.)

SCOTT. No! I wouldn't consider any such thing!

Then I asked him more questions about those three foreign missionaries. He seemed glad to talk about them. I asked if he'd ever visited any of the missions. No, he hadn't, but one of his sons and his daughter-in-law had charge of the mission in Nicaragua, and he was planning a trip to go down there and visit them in the autumn. Then he told me several stories about their work.

I listened with great interest. Later I asked: "Mr. Scott, when you go down to Nicaragua, wouldn't you be very happy to tell your son and his little family that you have just completed arrangements, making provision that, if anything happens to you, a check will come to them every month, so that their work may continue without interruption? And wouldn't you like to write a letter, Mr. Scott, to the other two missionaries, giving them the same message?"

Whenever he talked about it being too much money for him to pay out, I talked more, and asked more questions, about the wonderful work his foreign missionaries were doing.

Finally, he bought. He made a deposit that day of $8,672 to put the plan into action.

I walked out of that office—no, I didn't walk, I floated on air. I put the check in my side pocket, but held onto it with my hand. I was afraid to let go of it. I felt what a horrible nightmare it would be if I lost it before I got back to the office. I had a check for $8,672! Eight thousand, six hundred and seventy-two dollars! Only two years previously, I had been hoping to get a job as a shipping clerk. Truly, that sale gave me one of the biggest thrills of my life. When I reached the head office of my company I was astounded to hear that it was one of the biggest individual sales that had ever been made in their history.

I couldn't eat that night. I was awake until almost morning. It was August 3, 1920. I shall never forget the date. I was the most excited man in Philadelphia.

Since the sale was made by a green, blundering dub like

me, who had never finished grade school, it created a mild sensation. A few weeks later, I was invited to tell the story at a national sales convention in Boston.

Following my talk at the convention, a nationally known salesman, Clayton M. Hunsicker, a man nearly twice my age, came up and shook my hand, congratulating me on the sale. Then he told me something that I soon learned was the most profound secret of dealing with people.

Said he: "I still doubt whether you understand exactly *why* you were able to make that sale."

I asked him what he meant.

He then uttered the most vital truth I have ever heard about selling. He said: "The most important secret of salesmanship is to find out what the other fellow wants, then help him find the best way to get it. In the first minute of your interview with that man Scott, you took a blind stab, and accidentally found what he wanted. Then you showed him *how* he could get it. You kept on talking more about it, and asking more questions about it, never letting him get away from the thing he wanted. If you will always remember this one rule, selling will be easy."

All during the remainder of my three days' stay in Boston, I could think of little else except what Mr. Hunsicker had said. He was right. I hadn't really figured out *why* I had been able to make that sale. If Clayt Hunsicker hadn't analyzed it and interpreted it for me, I might have gone on stumbling through the years. As I thought over what he said, I began to understand why I had been meeting with such terrific opposition in most of my interviews. I realized that I was just barging in, talking for a sale, without knowing or trying to find out anything about the other fellow's situation.

I got so excited about this new idea I had used unknowingly, I could hardly wait until I got back to Philadelphia to use it.

All this started me thinking more about John Scott and his situation. Suddenly it occurred to me that he had *another* job to take care of, planning the future of his business. He had gone into great detail with me about how he came to America from Ireland as a lad of seventeen, took a job in a small grocery store, finally started his own business and gradually built one of the finest wholesale grocery businesses in the East. Naturally he had a sentimental feeling for that business. It was his life work. Surely he wanted it to continue long after he passed away.

Within thirty days after I returned from the Boston convention, I helped John Scott work out a plan to take his sons and eight other employees into the business with him. This was climaxed by a dinner which he gave at the Manufacturers' Club in Philadelphia for these key men. I was the only outside guest invited. Mr. Scott stood up after dinner, and in a brief, emotional talk, told his men what a happy occasion this was for him. "I have now completed plans for the future of the two things closest to my heart, my business and the foreign missions which I founded."

The insurance I placed on the lives of all these key men in the business, including additional amounts on Mr. Scott, resulted in a sale paying me more money in *one day* than I had ever earned previously in an entire year of selling.

The night of that dinner, I realized with full force how valuable a lesson Clayt Hunsicker had taught me. Before this, I had largely thought of selling as just a way of making a living for myself. I had dreaded to go in to see people, for I feared I was making a nuisance of myself. But now, I was inspired! I resolved right then to dedicate the rest of my selling career to this principle:

Finding out what people want, and helping them get it.

I can't begin to tell you the new kind of courage and en‐ thusiasm this gave me. Here was something more than a sales technique. It was a philosophy to live by.

6. HITTING THE BULL'S-EYE

❦ ⫷⫸ ⫷⫸

ONE THING that surprised me at that convention in Boston, was the large number of the nation's leading salesmen in attendance. Some of them had traveled all the way from California, Texas, and Florida.

I asked my new friend Mr. Hunsicker about this.

"Listen," he said, in a confidential way, "these top salesmen are all hungry for new ideas and always hunting for ways to do their job better. Attend as many sales conventions as you can. If you get only *one* idea, the time and money you spend will be the best investment you'll ever make. Besides, it will give you an opportunity to meet some of the big fellows. Meeting them personally and hearing them talk will inspire you. You'll go back home with a new confidence and enthusiasm."

This advice certainly worked out for me on that trip. Mr. Hunsicker himself was one of those big fellows, and the one idea he gave me was priceless. No wonder I had been missing the target so often. I didn't even know what the target was! In baseball they say: "You can't hit 'em if you don't see 'em." After Clayt Hunsicker showed me the target

44

I went home and really began shooting at the bull's-eye.

A couple of years later at a convention in Cleveland, a speaker whose name I've long since forgotten made a powerful talk on what he called "Rule One of Salesmanship." One example he used has always stayed with me. Here it is:

One night one of the main buildings of the Wooster University burned to the ground. Two days later, Louis E. Holden, young President of the University, went to see Andrew Carnegie.

Coming immediately to the point, Louis Holden said: "Mr. Carnegie, you are a busy man, and so am I. I won't take more than five minutes of your time. The main building of Wooster University burned down night before last, and I want you to give $100,000 for a new one."

Carnegie said: "Young man, I don't believe in giving money to colleges."

Holden replied: "But you believe in helping young men, don't you? I am a young man, Mr. Carnegie, and I am in an awful hole. I have gone into the business of manufacturing college men from raw material, and now the best part of my plant is gone. You know how you would feel if one of your big steel mills was destroyed, right in the busy season."

Carnegie: "Young man, raise $100,000 in thirty days, and I will give you another hundred."

Holden: "Make it sixty days and I will go you."

Carnegie: "Done."

Picking up his hat, Dr. Holden started for the door. Mr. Carnegie called after him. "Now remember, it's sixty days only."

"All right, sir, I understand," answered Holden.

Louis Holden's interview had taken just about *four minutes.* Within fifty days he raised $100,000.

When handing over his check, Andrew Carnegie said, laughing, "Young man, if you ever come to see me again, don't stay so long. Your call cost me just $25,000 a minute."

Louis Holden had shot straight for the bull's-eye. He knew one of the tenderest spots in Mr. Carnegie's heart was for ambitious young men.

Dr. Holden probably had much to do with selling an idea far bigger than raising $100,000 for Wooster University. Andrew Carnegie finally gave away more than $100,000,000 for the advancement of education.

Applying this rule: Try *to find out what people want, and then help them get it.* That is the one big secret of selling anything.

Just recently I saw a superb demonstration of the wrong and the right way to apply this rule. I was in a large Western city at the time when a man we'll call Brown phoned me at the hotel. He said: "Mr. Bettger, my name is Brown. I am going to promote a sales school here in the city for young salesmen, and I am hoping we can get started next month. I am holding a mass meeting tonight at the hotel where you are stopping. We have spent considerable money advertising the meeting, and I believe there will be a crowd of several hundred people. I would very much appreciate it if you would give us a little talk. We will have several other speakers, so you won't have to talk longer than about ten minutes. I have learned from experience that unless I can form a large class out of this meeting, it is a losing proposition, so I sure would be grateful to you for your help . . . etc. . . . etc."

I didn't know this man Brown. Why should I go out of my way to help him promote *his* project? I was busy with plenty of things I wanted to do for myself. Besides, I was getting ready to leave the following day. So I wished him success but asked him to please let me off because of the extreme inconvenience to me right at that time.

Later in the day, however, another man phoned whom we'll call White. He was calling me about exactly the same project. Let's listen in on his approach:

"Mr. Bettger, my name is White—Joe White. I understand Mr. Brown has already told you about our opening meeting this evening at the hotel. I know how busy you must be getting ready to leave, but if there is any way you could possibly arrange to be with us for a few minutes, Mr. Bettger, you could do a lot of good. I know you are interested in helping young people, and our audience will be largely made up of young salesmen, ambitious to improve themselves and get ahead. You know how much this same training would have meant to you when you were trying to get started. I don't know of *anyone*, Mr. Bettger, who could do more good at a meeting of this kind than you!"

The first man made the same mistake that I had been making (and might have kept right on making all the rest of my life if it hadn't been for Clayt Hunsicker), he talked about himself, and his proposition, and what *he* wanted. The second man never once referred to what *he* wanted. He shot straight for the bull's-eye. He appealed to me entirely from *my* viewpoint. I found it impossible to say "No" to this second kind of appeal.

Dale Carnegie says: "There is only one way under high heaven to get anybody to do anything. Did you ever stop to think of that? Yes, just one way. And that is by making the other person *want* to do it. Remember, there is no other way."

Just before World War II, I was giving a series of lectures in several Western cities. Invariably, after I spoke on this subject, a few men would come up to ask questions. One night in Des Moines, Iowa, a middle-aged man said: "Mr. Bettger, I can see how this idea has been a great help to you in selling life insurance, but I solicit subscriptions for a nationally known magazine. How could I apply it in *my* work?"

He and I had a frank discussion. This man had tried selling various lines for several years and obviously had grown very cynical. After I suggested a different method of approach to him, he left, but I didn't feel that he was very enthusiastic about our interview.

The following Saturday morning I was having my hair cut in the Hotel Fort Des Moines barber shop when the man rushed in and said he heard that I was leaving on an early afternoon train but he just *had* to tell me something.

"After your talk on Tuesday night, Mr. Bettger," he said, with surprising excitement, "I realized why I wasn't getting anywhere. I had been trying to sell magazines to business men, but most of them told me they were so busy they didn't have time to read the magazines they already subscribed to.

On Wednesday I succeeded in obtaining a letter from one of the most prominent judges in the city saying that he takes our magazine because it gives him all the really important and interesting news of the week *in one short evening of reading*. Then I procured a large list of prominent business men in the city who are already subscribers. Now, Mr. Bettger, when I approach a man, I show him the judge's letter and this list. The very objection which has been stopping me is now my biggest asset. What I am trying to tell you is that I am no longer peddling *magazines;* I'm selling business men something they all want. I'm selling the most precious thing in life—*more time*."

Only a few days before, this salesman felt that most of the people he called on looked down on him. He dreaded to go in to see people. Now he had an entirely new outlook on the importance of the work he was doing.

Here was the *same man,* selling the *same product,* in the *same city,* succeeding, where he had previously been failing.

As I have told you, a number of years ago I was elected superintendent of a small Sunday school. I thought the important immediate need of the school was for a larger organization, so I asked the pastor to give me five minutes' time on the program at the following Sunday morning church service. I knew I had to make a sale. Now, I *could* have got up and told the congregation that this job had been wished on me and I would expect them to cooperate and help me, but I decided that I would have a much better chance of getting what *I* wanted, if I talked to them about what *they* wanted. So here is what I did say:

"I want to talk to you for just a few minutes about some of the things you want. Many of you have children. You want them to come here to Sunday school and meet other nice children and to learn more about life from the truths in the great Book. You and I want our children to avoid some of the mistakes that I have made, and possibly some you have made. How can we do this?

"The only way we can do it is by building a larger organization. You now have only nine teachers in the Sunday school, including the pastor himself. We need at least twenty-five. Some of you may hesitate to teach because you have the same fears that I had only twelve months ago when I took a small class of boys—that you don't know enough about the Bible. Well, I can tell you, you'll learn more about this Book in six months by teaching these little children for twenty minutes each Sunday morning than you will ever learn in six years by merely listening—and it will do more for *you!*

"You husbands and wives can study and prepare the lessons together. It will give you something more in common, bring you closer together. If you have children of your own, they too will take a greater interest when they see you active. Remember Jesus' parable about the three men who were given the talents? You men and women have been given many talents. I don't know of any better way you can improve and multiply your talents than through this work."

What happened? That morning, we got twenty-one new teachers. At first there were not enough children to go around, but we divided them up. Some classes started off with only two and three. Then we put on a house-to-house canvass. We enrolled all but three of the Protestant children in the community of Wynnefield, Pennsylvania. Finally the little chapel wouldn't hold all the members, so we had to build a new church! And in a three months' campaign, the people of the Wynnefield United Presbyterian Church raised $180,000, contributed by some 372 men, women, and children.

Those teachers were certainly not entirely responsible for this amazing record, but the fact is, it couldn't have happened if it hadn't been for the growth of the Bible school.

When you show a man what he wants, he'll move heaven and earth to get it.

This universal law is of such paramount importance that it takes precedence over all other laws of human relations. It always *has* been, and always will be the most important. Yes, it looms up as Rule Number One over all other rules in civilization.

Benjamin Franklin understood the importance of this law. He even formed a prayer that helped him get it down into his heart. When I first began reading Franklin's autobiography, I was interested to discover that he had been saying the same prayer every day for fifty years. I live in Philadelphia, the town where Benjamin Franklin spent most of his life, and he has always been an inspiration to me.

I said to myself, "If that prayer helped Ben Franklin, it certainly ought to help me"—so I have been saying the prayer for more than twenty-five years. It helped me get my mind off myself and what I was going to make out of a sale, and get my mind on the other person and what *he* would get out of the sale. Franklin wrote: " . . . and conceiving God to be the fountain of wisdom, I thought it right and necessary to solicit His assistance for obtaining it; to this end, I formed the following prayer which was prefixed to my tables of examination for daily use."

Here is the prayer—Ben Franklin's prayer:

O powerful Goodness! bountiful Father! merciful Guide! Increase in me that wisdom which discovers my truest interest. Strengthen my resolutions to perform what that wisdom dictates. Accept my kind offices to Thy other children as the only return in my power for Thy continual favors to me.

SUMMED UP

1. The most important secret of salesmanship is to find out what the other fellow wants, then help him find the best way to get it.

2. There is only one way under heaven to get anybody to do anything. Did you ever think of that? Yes, just one way. And that is by making the other person want to do it. Remember, there is no other way.

3. When you show a man what he *wants,* he will move heaven and earth to get it.

7. A $250,000 SALE IN
◆ FIFTEEN MINUTES

→⟩⟩ ⟨⟨←

AFTER Clayt Hunsicker took me aside up in Boston and taught me the big secret of selling, my enthusiasm reached a new, all-time high. I thought all I had to do now was go out and see enough people—and selling would be easy!

During the next few months my sales record *did* show a definite improvement, but still I kept meeting with too much opposition. I couldn't understand why.

Then one day, while attending a sales congress at the Bellevue-Stratford Hotel in Philadelphia, I heard one of America's top salesmen reveal an amazing method that gave me the answer in a nutshell. He was J. Elliott Hall, of New York City. Although he has been retired now for several years, Elliott Hall's record still stands among the all-time top producers.

Mr. Hall told how he had failed as a salesman and was about to quit when he discovered the reason *why* he was failing. He said he had been making too many "positive statements."

To me, this sounded silly.

But he then electrified that large audience by throwing the meeting wide open to objections and answers. Two thousand salesmen began firing objections at him from all directions—objections that prospects and customers had been "brushing 'em off" with every day.

The excitement became terrific as Elliott Hall gave a super-demonstration of how he met these objections—not with smart stock answers found in books written about "How to Meet Objections." He met these objections by *asking questions.*

He didn't attempt to tell his objectors that they were wrong, and show them how much smarter he was than they. He simply asked questions with which his objectors had to agree. And he kept on asking questions until the answers added up to just *one* conclusion—a sound conclusion based on facts.

The profound lesson I learned from that master salesman changed my whole way of thinking. He never gave the impression that he was trying to persuade or influence anybody to *his* way of thinking. Elliott Hall's questions had only one purpose:

> *To help the other fellow recognize what he wants, then help him decide how to get it.*

One of the toughest objections to overcome, the audience told Mr. Hall, was: "I haven't made up my mind whether I'm going to take it or not."

"My job," answered Mr. Hall, "is to help the customer in making up his mind. There is no question in the world as to whether or not . . ." Then, he'd sum it all up with questions.

"*I want to go home and think it over,*" one salesman said was his big stumbling block.

"I am going to find out if we can help you to think it over," answered Mr. Hall. "You don't *have* to think over the . . ." Back went Mr. Hall to his questions, in order to help his objector find just what it *was* he wanted to think over.

Even with all of his persistence no one got the impression that Elliott Hall was arguing or contradicting anybody. He was extremely forceful, yet never once did he *argue,* or contradict, or offer a fixed opinion of his own. His attitude was not that of "I know I'm right; you're wrong."

His method of helping people to crystallize their thinking —with questions—continues to be without parallel in my experience. I shall never forget him and the substance of what he said.

As I listened, pop-eyed, to Elliott Hall that day, I resolved that, from then on, I would make it a major ambition of mine to try to cultivate this great art which he had mastered to such a high degree—the art of asking questions.

A few days after Mr. Hall's talk, a friend of mine called me on the phone and said that a large New York manufacturer was in the market for $250,000 of life insurance. He wanted to know if I'd be interested in submitting a proposition. This manufacturer's company was borrowing $250,000, and the creditors were insisting on that amount of insurance on the life of the president. About ten large companies of

New York had already submitted elaborate proposals.

"Sure I'll be interested in submitting a proposition," I said, "if you can arrange an appointment for me."

Later that day my friend phoned that he had succeeded in arranging an interview for the following morning at ten forty-five. Here's what happened:

First I sat there at my desk thinking what to do. Elliott Hall's talk was still fresh in my mind. I decided to prepare a series of questions. For half an hour my mind just ran around in circles. Then some questions began to pop—questions that should help this man crystallize his thinking and aid him in making a decision. It took me nearly two hours. Finally I had written down fourteen questions at random. These I rearranged in more logical sequence.

The next morning on the train going to New York, I studied the questions over and over. By the time I arrived in Pennsylvania Station, I was so excited I could hardly wait for the interview. To strengthen my confidence, I decided to take a long chance. I phoned one of New York's biggest medical examiners, and arranged an appointment for my prospective customer at the examiner's office for 11:30 A.M.

Arriving at my prospect's office, I was greeted by his secretary. She opened the president's door and I heard her say, "Mr. Booth, there's a Mr. Bettger from Philadelphia here to see you. He says he has an appointment with you for ten forty-five."

BOOTH. Oh, yes. Send him in.
ME. Mr. Booth!

BOOTH. How do you do, Mr. Bettger. Have a seat. (*Mr. Booth waited for me to talk, but I waited for him.*)   Mr. Bettger, I'm afraid you're wasting your time.

ME. Why?

BOOTH *(pointing to stack of proposals and illustrations on desk)*. I've had plans submitted to me by all of the leading New York companies, three of which were presented by friends of mine—one of them a close personal friend; I play golf with him every Saturday and Sunday. He's with the New York Life; that's a pretty good company, isn't it?

ME. None better in the world!

BOOTH. Well, Mr. Bettger, under the circumstances, if you still feel that you want to submit a proposition to me, you can make up figures for $250,000 of insurance on the ordinary life plan at my age, forty-six, and just *mail* it to me. I will put it with these other proposals and sometime during the next couple of weeks, I expect to reach a decision. If your plan is the cheapest and the best, you will get the business. But I think you are just wasting your time and my time.

ME. Mr. Booth, if you were my own brother, I would say to you what I'm going to say to you now.

BOOTH. What's that?

ME. Knowing what I do about the insurance business, if you were my own brother, I would tell you to take all those proposals and immediately throw them into that waste paper basket.

BOOTH (*obviously astonished*). Why do you say that?

ME. Well, in the first place, properly to interpret those

proposals would require an actuary, and it takes seven years to become an actuary. But even if you were able to select the lowest-cost proposition today, five years from now that very company could be among the highest-cost companies of this group. That is history. Frankly, those companies you have selected are the best in the world. You could take all those proposals, spread them over the top of your desk, close your eyes, and the one you happen to point at could just as likely be the lowest-cost company, as the one you would carefully choose after *weeks* of deliberation. Now, Mr. Booth, my job is to help you arrive at a final decision. In order to help you do this, I must ask you some questions. Is that all right?

BOOTH. Sure. Go right ahead.

ME. As I understand it, your company is to be extended a running line of credit of a quarter of a million dollars. Part of the deal is that your life is to be insured for $250,000, the policies to be assigned to your creditors. Is that right?

BOOTH. Yes. That is right.

ME. In other words, they have confidence in *you,* if you live, but in the event of your death, they don't have the same confidence in your company. Isn't that right, Mr. Booth?

BOOTH. Yes, I suppose that's right.

ME. Then why isn't it of paramount importance—in fact the *only* thing of importance—that you obtain this insurance immediately and transfer that risk to the insurance companies? Suppose you should wake up tonight, in the middle of the night, and it should suddenly occur to you that the fire insurance on your large plant up in Connecticut had expired yesterday. Why you probably wouldn't be able to get back to sleep the rest of the night! And the first thing tomorrow morning you would have your broker on the phone telling him to protect you immediately, wouldn't you?

BOOTH. Of course I would.

ME. Well, your creditors regard this insurance on your life with just the same importance that you regard the fire insurance on your plant. Isn't it possible that if anything developed whereby you would be unable to obtain this insurance on your life, your creditors might reduce or even entirely refuse to grant you this loan?

BOOTH. Oh, I don't know, but I suppose that's quite possible.

ME. And if you should find yourself unable to obtain this credit, wouldn't it probably mean thousands and thousands of dollars to you? Wouldn't it probably mean the difference between a profit and a loss to your business this year?

BOOTH. Yes. I suppose that is true.

ME. Mr. Booth, I am in a position to do something for you this morning that no other living person can do for you!

BOOTH. What do you mean by that?

ME. I have an appointment for you this morning at eleven thirty with Dr. Carlyle, one of the leading medical examiners of New York City. His examination is recognized by practically all the life insurance companies. He is the only medical examiner I know whose single examination is good for $250,000 of insurance on one person's life. He has electrocardiograph and fluoroscope machines and all the other equipment necessary for such an examination as you require right in his office at 150 Broadway.

BOOTH. Can't these other brokers do the same thing for me?

ME. Not this morning they can't! Mr. Booth, recognizing the serious importance of having this examination made immediately, suppose you should telephone one of these brokers this afternoon and tell him to proceed at once. The first thing he would do would be to phone one of his friends, a regular examiner, and try to have him here in your office this afternoon to make the first examination. If the doctor's papers were mailed out tonight, one of the medical directors for that particular company would sit at his desk at the head office tomorrow morning looking at you on paper. If he decided that you were a quarter-of-a-million-dollar risk, he would then authorize a second examination by another doctor who would have the necessary equipment. This all means further delay. Why should you take this risk for another week, even another day?

BOOTH. Oh, I think I'm going to live a while.

ME. Suppose you should wake up tomorrow morning with a sore throat and find yourself laid up for a week with the grippe? Then when you were well enough to have this difficult examination made the insurance company would say to you: "Now, Mr. Booth, we think you are going to be all right again, but there is some little condition which has developed as a result of your recent illness, and we must postpone action for three or four months until we find whether it is temporary, or something permanent." You would then have to tell your creditors that the final judgment was post-poned. Isn't it possible that they would postpone the extension of this loan to you? Isn't that a *possibility*, Mr. Booth?"

BOOTH. Yes, of course that's a possibility.

ME (*looking at my watch*). Mr. Booth, it is now eleven ten. If we leave here immediately, we will be able to keep that appointment with Dr. Carlyle in his office at eleven thirty. You look as though you never felt better in your life. If you are as good on the inside as you look on the outside, you should be able to have this insurance in effect in forty-eight hours. You *are* feeling well this morning, aren't you, Mr. Booth?

BOOTH. Yes, I'm feeling very well.

ME. Then why isn't this examination the most important thing in the world for you to take care of right now?

BOOTH. Mr. Bettger, whom do you represent?

ME. I represent you!

BOOTH (*bowing head in thought. Lights cigarette. After a few moments slowly rises from desk, looks into space, walks over to window, then to hatrack. Takes hat off rack and turns to me*). Let's go!

We rode down to the doctor's office on the Sixth Avenue subway. After the examination was satisfactorily completed, Mr. Booth seemed suddenly to become my friend. He insisted on taking me to lunch with him. As we began eating, he looked at me and began to laugh. "By the way," he asked, "what company *do* you represent?"

8. ANALYSIS OF THE BASIC PRINCIPLES USED IN MAKING THAT ◆ SALE

※ ※

LET'S analyze that sale. Now I know what you are think-ing. You are saying to yourself: "How can *I* use this technique? That may be all right for you. That sold insurance, but how can I use it?" Well you can use this same technique in selling "shoes and ships and sealing-wax," and here's how you can do it:

1. MAKE APPOINTMENTS.

Be expected! You gain a big advantage when you make an appointment. It tells the other person you appreciate the value of *his* time. Unconsciously, he places more impor-tance on the value of *your* time. I never would have had a chance if I had gone to New York to see that busy executive *without an appointment.*

2. BE PREPARED.

What would you do if you were invited to speak before a joint meeting of the Junior and Senior Chambers of Com-merce and all the other service clubs in your community, and they were going to pay you $100? You'd spend many hours preparing, wouldn't you? You'd sit up nights plan-ning exactly how you would open your talk; points you

63

wanted to cover; your close. You'd treat it as an event, wouldn't you? Why? Because you would have an audience of three or four hundred or more. Well, don't forget, there is no difference between an audience of four hundred, and an audience of one. And it may mean *more* than $100 to you. Over a period of years, it may mean several hundred dollars to you. So why not treat each interview as an event?

After I got that phone call from my friend saying he had arranged an appointment for the following morning, I sat at my desk for probably thirty minutes, wondering what I would say to this man. Nothing I could think of appealed to me. "Well," I thought, "I'm tired now. I'll do it tomorrow morning on the way over on the train."

Then that small voice whispered in my ear: "Tomorrow morning, nothing! *You'll do it right now!* You know how you lack confidence when you go out unprepared. This man has agreed to an appointment with you, Bettger. Let's *prepare!* And go over there with a winning attitude!"

After a while this question came to me: "What is the key issue?" That wasn't hard to answer. Credit. This silk manufacturer must have credit. His creditors insist on his life being insured. Every day, every hour he delays action in obtaining this insurance, he takes a big risk. Net cost of the insurance really isn't important at all.

This simple little idea has proved to be a constant help to me in preparing for an interview or a speech. I get started right if I first ask myself this question:

3 WHAT IS THE KEY ISSUE?

Or, what is the major point of interest?

Or, what is the most vulnerable point?

That's what won that business for me in competition with ten other large companies.

Listen to what Mr. Booth said to me while we sat eating lunch that day:

"I suppose some of my insurance friends are going to get a big shock. But they have been pushing me around for weeks, knocking each other, and trying to show me how much cheaper their plan would be. You didn't knock anybody, but you made me realize the risk I was taking by waiting"—then, with a grin—"In fact, I became terrified thinking of the possibility of losing that credit. I decided it would be just stupid if I even went out to lunch *before* I had that examination made."

That sale taught me a big lesson: Never try to cover too many points; don't obscure the main issue; find out what it is, then stay right on the beam.

4. KEY WORD NOTES.

It is an unusual person who can go into an interview, conference, or even make an important telephone call, and

(a) Remember points he wants to cover.

(b) Cover them in logical order.

(c) Be brief and stay on the main point.

Unless I first make notes, I'm likely to fall down badly here. In preparing for the Booth interview, I made key word notes. On my way over on the train I reviewed these notes again and again, until I knew exactly what I was going to say, and how I was going to say it. That gave me confidence. I never once had to refer to my notes during the interview. However, if my memory fails me when interviewing people I do not hesitate to pull out my card of key word notes.

5. ASK QUESTIONS.

Of the fourteen questions I had prepared the day before, I actually used eleven. In fact, this entire fifteen-minute interview consisted largely of questions and answers. The importance of *asking questions* is such a vital subject, and has been such a big factor in whatever success I've had in selling, that I am devoting the whole next chapter to it.

6. EXPLODE DYNAMITE!

Do something startling, surprising. It is often necessary to arouse people and stir them to action for their own benefit. You'd better not do it, however, unless you are prepared to back up the explosion with facts, not opinions.

I said to Mr. Booth: "Knowing what I do about the insurance business, if you were my own brother, I would tell you to take all those proposals and immediately throw them into that waste paper basket!"

7. AROUSE FEAR.

Basically, there are only two factors that move men to action: desire for gain, and fear of loss. Advertising men tell us that fear is the most motivating factor where risk or danger is involved. The entire talk to Mr. Booth was based on *fear* and the unnecessary risk he was taking of losing $250,000 of credit.

8. CREATE CONFIDENCE.

If you are absolutely sincere, there are many ways you can create confidence with people. I believe there were four rules that helped me gain this stranger's confidence:

(a) Be an Assistant Buyer.

In preparation for the interview, I imagined myself a salaried employee of Mr. Booth's company. I assumed the role of "assistant buyer in charge of insurance." In this matter my knowledge was superior to Mr. Booth's. Feeling this way, I didn't hesitate to put all the enthusiasm and excitement I could command into what I said. That idea helped me to be absolutely fearless. The assistant buyer attitude was such a definite help to me in that sale that I have kept right on through the years playing that role. I would urge any young man selling, or dealing with people, to become an assistant buyer. People don't like to be sold. They like to buy.

(b) "If you were my own brother, I'd say to you what I'm going to say to you now. . . ."

A powerful confidence-gainer, if you can use it with absolute sincerity. These were almost the first words I spoke to Mr. Booth. I looked him steadily in the eye and spoke them with feeling. Then I waited for him to say something. He asked the question most prospects do: "What is that?"

(c) Praise Your Competitors.

"If you can't boost, don't knock" is *always* a safe rule. I've found it is one of the quickest confidence-gainers. Try to say something good about the other fellow. When Mr. Booth spoke about having a friend with the New York Life,

he said, "That's a pretty good company, isn't it?" I quickly
replied: "None better in the world!" Then, right back to
my questions.

> (d) "I am in a position to do something for you this
> morning that no other living person can do for
> you."

A powerful selling phrase. Where it honestly fits, it has
surprising effect. Let me give one example:

As Dale Carnegie and I were getting ready to board the
train one evening in Des Moines, Iowa, Russell Levine, a
live-wire member of the Junior Chamber of Commerce,
sponsors of our school, came down to the station to say
goodbye. Russell said: "One of your phrases sold a whole
freight car of oil for me yesterday." I said: "Tell me
about it."

Russell replied that he had called on a customer yesterday
and had said: "I am in a position to do something for you
this morning that no other living person can do for you."

"What is that?" the customer asked, surprised.

"I can get you a whole freight carload of oil," Russell said.

"No," said the customer.

"Why not?" Russell asked.

"I wouldn't have any place to put it," the man answered.

"Mr. D.," Russell said earnestly, "if you were my own
brother, I'd say to you what I am going to say to you now."

"What's that?" the customer asked.

"Take this carload of oil now. There is going to be a
shortage, and you won't be able to get what you need later.
Besides, there's going to be a big advance in price."

"No," the man repeated, "I have no space here for it."

"Rent a storage place," Russell suggested.

"No," he said, "I'll have to pass it up."

Later in the day when Russell returned to his office there was a message to call this man. When Russell got him on the phone he said, "Russell, I've rented an old garage where I can store that oil, so you've sold me the carload!'

9. EXPRESS HONEST APPRECIATION OF YOUR LISTENER'S ABILITY.

Everyone likes to feel important. People are hungry for praise. People are starving for honest appreciation. But we don't have to go overboard. It is much more effective to be conservative with it. I know it pleased this successful business man when I pointed out to him: "They have confidence in *you,* if you live, but in the event of your death, they don't have the same confidence in your company. Isn't that right, Mr. Booth?"

10. ASSUME A CLOSE.

Have a winning attitude. I took the gamble of making an appointment with Dr. Carlyle before I ever saw my prospect. I put all my chips on a winner.

11. PUT YOU IN THE INTERVIEW

Years later after I began to learn more about basic principles, I analyzed this sale and was surprised to find that I had used the word "you" or "yours" *sixty-nine* times in that short fifteen-minute interview. I don't remember where I first heard of this test but it is a superb way for you to make certain you are practicing the most important rule of all:

See things from the other person's point of view
and talk in terms of his wants, needs, desires.

Would you like to try a highly interesting and profitable test on yourself? Write out what you said in your last selling interview. Then see how many places you can find to strike out the personal pronoun "I," or "we," and change it to "you" or "your." Put *you* in the interview.

9. HOW ASKING QUESTIONS INCREASED THE EFFECTIVENESS OF MY SALES INTERVIEWS

→⟩⟩ ⟨⟨←

A NEW idea sometimes produces rapid and revolutionary changes in a man's thinking. For instance, only a short time before I made that sale in New York, I had set a goal for myself to become a "quarter-million-dollar-a-year producer." I thought that by hard, consistent work, I could make it.

Now, suddenly, I produced a quarter-million in *one day!* Fantastic! How could this be? Only one week before, a quarter-million a year looked big. Now, here I was thinking "a *million* is my goal!"

Those were some of the thoughts racing through my head that night on the train riding back to Philadelphia. I was having an emotional jag. I was too excited to stay in my seat. Back and forth I paced through the car. Every seat was occupied, but I don't remember seeing a soul. Over and over again I went through the sale. Every word of it. What Mr. Booth said. What I said. Finally I sat down and wrote out the entire interview.

"How utterly futile and ridiculous that trip would have been," I said to myself, "if I hadn't heard that talk Elliott

Hall gave on the importance of asking questions." The truth is, just a few days before I wouldn't even have considered going to New York on such a case.

I realized this: If I had attempted to say exactly the same things without putting them in the form of questions, I'd have been kicked out in three minutes flat! Although I said what I had to say with all the force and excitement I possibly could, this successful manufacturer never once showed any resentment. Putting my ideas in the form of questions showed him how I felt about what he should do, but at the same time kept him in the buyer's seat. Each time he offered an objection or comment, I passed the ball right back to him with another question. When he finally got up, took his hat and said: "Let's go!" I know he felt that the idea was his.

Only a few days later I obtained a letter of introduction from a friend of mine to the young president of a firm of building engineers who were then erecting several important projects. It was one of the most promising organizations in the city.

The young president read my letter of introduction at a glance, and said: "If it's insurance you want to talk about, I'm not interested. I just bought more insurance about a month ago."

There was something so final in his manner, I felt as though it would be fatal to be persistent. However I was sincere in wanting to know this man better, so I ventured one question:

"Mr. Allen, how did you ever happen to get started in the building construction business?"

I listened for three hours.

Finally his secretary came in with some checks for him to sign. As she left the young executive looked up at me but said nothing. I looked back at him in silence.

"What do you want me to do?" he asked.

"I want you to answer a few questions," I replied.

I left there knowing exactly what was in his mind—his hopes, ambitions, objectives. Once during the interview he said, "I don't know why I'm telling you all these things. You know more now than I've ever told anybody—even my wife!"

I believe he discovered things that day he didn't know himself; things that had never definitely crystallized in his own mind.

I thanked him for his confidence and told him I was going to give some thought and study to the information he had given me. Two weeks later I presented a plan to him and his two associates for the perpetuation and protection of their business. It was Christmas Eve. I left that company's office at four o'clock that afternoon with signed orders for $100,000 insurance on the life of the president; $100,000 on the vice-president; and $25,000 on the secretary-treasurer.

That was the beginning of a close personal friendship with these men. During the following ten years, the business I did with them increased to a total of three-quarters of a million dollars.

Never once have I felt that I've "sold" them anything. They've always "bought." Instead of trying to give them the impression that I knew all the answers—as was my habit before I heard J. Elliott Hall—*I made them give me the answers,* largely by asking questions.

For a quarter of a century I've found this way of handling people a hundred times more effective than trying to win them to *my* way of thinking.

At the time I got this idea from Mr. Hall I thought he had discovered a new way of thinking. Shortly afterward I learned that another great salesman, right here in Philadelphia, took some time out to write a few things on this subject 150 years before I met Mr. Hall. You may have heard of him. His name was Benjamin Franklin.

Franklin told how he dug up this idea from a man who lived in Athens, Greece, 2,200 years before Ben Franklin himself was born. That man's name was Socrates. By *his* method of questioning, Socrates did something that few men in all history have been able to do—he changed the thinking of the world.

I was surprised to learn that, as a young man, Franklin couldn't get along with people, made enemies because he argued, made so many positive statements, tried to dominate people. Finally, he came to realize that he was losing out all around. Then he became interested in studying the Socratic method. He took great delight in developing this art and practiced it continually.

"This habit," Franklin wrote, "I believe has been of great advantage to me when I have had occasion to persuade men into measures that I have been from time to time engaged in promoting; and as the chief ends of conversation are to inform or to be informed, I wish well-meaning, sensible men would not lessen their power of doing good by a positive, assuming manner, that tends to create opposition and to defeat every one of those purposes for which speech was given us."

Franklin grew very artful and expert in drawing people out; but he found the following simple rule most important in *preparing* the other person for his questions:

"When another asserted something that I thought in error, I deny'd myself the pleasure of contradicting him abruptly, and of showing immediately some absurdity in his propositions; and in answering I began by observing that *in certain cases or circumstances his opinion would be right, but in the present case there appear'd or seem'd to me some difference*, etc. I soon found the advantage of this change in my manner; the conversation I engaged in went on more pleasantly. The modest way in which I propos'd my opinions procur'd them a readier reception and less contradiction; I had less mortification when I was found to be in the wrong and I more easily prevailed with others to give up their mistakes and join with me when I happened to be in the right."

This procedure seemed so practical and simple, I began trying it in selling. It helped me immediately. I merely paraphrased Franklin's words the best I could to fit the occasion.

I blush when I think of how I used to say: "I can't agree with you there because . . ."

The "don't you think" habit is a little aid which I find helps me avoid making so many positive statements. For example, if I say to you: "We should avoid making so many positive statements. We should ask more questions," I have merely stated *my* opinion. But if I say to you: *"Don't you think* we should avoid making so many positive statements? *Don't you feel* we should ask more questions?" haven't I shown you how I feel? But haven't I, at the same time, made you happier by asking your opinion? Isn't your listener likely to have ten times as much enthusiasm if he thinks the idea is his?

You can do *two* things with a question:
1. Let the other person know what you think.
2. You can at the same time pay him the compliment of asking his opinion.

A famous educator once said to me: "One of the biggest things you get out of a college education is a questioning attitude, a habit of demanding and weighing evidence . . . a scientific approach."

Well I never had the advantage of going to college but I know one of the best ways to get men to think is to ask them questions. Pertinent questions. In fact, I have found in many cases, it is the *only* way to get them to think!

SIX THINGS YOU GAIN BY THE
QUESTION METHOD

1. Helps you to avoid arguments.
2. Helps you avoid talking too much.
3. Enables you to help the other fellow recognize what he wants. Then you can help him decide how to get it.
4. Helps crystallize the other person's thinking. The idea becomes *his* idea.
5. Helps you find the most vulnerable point with which to close the sale—the key issue.
6. Gives the other person a feeling of importance. When you show that you respect his opinion, he is more likely to respect yours.

"One of the biggest things you get out of a college education is a questioning attitude, a habit of demanding and weighing evidence . . . a scientific approach."

10. HOW I LEARNED TO FIND THE MOST IMPORTANT REASON WHY A MAN SHOULD BUY

⊱⊰

THERE was a story going around one time about a big, strong man in a New York night club who was offering to allow anybody in the audience to hit him in the stomach as hard as they could. Several men tried it, including Jack Dempsey, it was said, but the blows never seemed to faze the strong man. One night in the rear of the audience was a big, powerful Swede, who couldn't understand a word of English. Someone said he could strike a mighty blow. The master of ceremonies went back and finally made the Swede understand by pantomime that they wanted him to go up and hit the strong man. The Swede went up, took off his coat, and rolled up his sleeves. The strong man swelled up his chest with a deep breath, and braced himself for the blow. The Swede swung from the floor, but instead of striking him in the stomach, landed one right on the strong man's jaw and knocked him out.

Because of a misunderstanding of what he was supposed to do, that big Swede had unknowingly applied one of the major rules of selling. He picked out the most vulnerable

point and concentrated everything on that one point alone
—the key issue.

The prospect himself doesn't always realize what his vital
need is. Let's take the example of Mr. Booth, the silk manufacturer in New York. He thought that the key issue was
where he could get insurance at the lowest cost. He was
going to get down to the bottom of this thing. He had insurance men on his heels day and night. It was just like
everybody hitting the strong man in the stomach.

I found that by questioning him, I got his mind off what
he *thought* was the real issue, and got him on the track of
what was really the most vital issue of all.

The first thing I remember reading that made me stop
and think how important it is to find the key issue was something that Lincoln said: "Much of my success as a trial lawyer lay in the fact that I was always willing to give the
opposing attorney six points in order to gain the seventh—
if the seventh was the most important."

The Rock Island Railroad trial, to which we shall refer
later on, is a superb example of how Lincoln applied this
rule. On the closing day of the trial, the opposing lawyer
took two hours to sum up the case. Lincoln could have
taken time to argue several points that his opponent made.
But rather than risk confusing the jury, Lincoln waived all
but one thing—the key issue. That took him less than one
minute. But it won the case.

I have talked with thousands of salesmen, and find that
many of them pay no attention at all to the key issue. Oh,

yes, they have read about it. But what *is* the key issue?
Let's simplify it. Isn't it just this:

What is the basic need?
or
*What is the main point of interest, the most
vulnerable point?*

How can you get at the key issue? Encourage your prospect to talk. As soon as a man gives you four or five reasons
why he won't buy, and you try to argue each one, you aren't
going to sell him.

If you just get him to keep on talking, he will help you
sell him. Why? Because he will pick out of these four or
five things, the one thing that is the most important, and
stick to it. Sometimes, you don't have to say a word. When
he gets all through, come back to that one point. Usually,
that's the true one.

Several years ago, I attended a national sales convention
in Pittsburgh. William G. Power, public relations executive
of the Chevrolet motor company, told this story: "I was
about to buy a home in Detroit. I called in a real estate
man. He was one of the smartest salesmen I have ever met.
He listened as I talked, and after a while found out that all
my life I had wanted to own a tree. He drove me about
twelve miles from Detroit and into the back yard of a house
in a nicely wooded section. He said, 'Look at those gor-
geous trees, eighteen of them!'

"I looked at those trees, I admired them, and asked him

the price of the house. He said, 'X dollars.' I said, 'Get out your pencil and sharpen it.' He wouldn't shade the price a nickel. 'What are you talking about?' I said. 'I can buy a house just like that for less money.' He said: 'If you can, more power to you, but look at those trees—one . . . two . . . three . . . four . . .'

"Each time I talked price, he counted those trees. He sold me the eighteen trees . . . and threw in the house!

"That is salesmanship. He listened until he found out what I wanted, and then sold it to me."

I have walked away from many sales, just by letting a man take me all around Robin Hood's barn, and I have tried to answer them all in full. Then the telephone would ring and he would say, "I'm not going to do anything for a while." Gradually by trial and error, I have found the thing to do is to agree with everything he says until I find out what is the *real* reason he isn't buying.

Many prospects try to mislead you. In the next two chapters I will show how I use two simple little questions to determine whether an objection is real, and a method I've found so effective in bringing out the hidden reason.

SUMMED UP

The main problem in the sale is to
1. Find the basic need, or
2. The main point of interest.
3. Then stick to it!

11. THE MOST IMPORTANT WORD I HAVE FOUND IN SELLING HAS ONLY THREE LETTERS

➤➤➤   ◀◀◀

THE MOST powerful word in the English language, I believe, is the little word *why*—but it took me years of stupid stumbling to find it out. Before I learned the importance of this little one-word question, whenever a man offered an objection, I immediately argued the point with him.

It wasn't until one day when a friend of mine telephoned me and invited me to have lunch with him, that I really appreciated the power of this miracle-performing word. My friend's name is James C. Walker, president and principal owner of Gibson-Walker Lumber Company, F and Luzerne Streets, Philadelphia. After we ordered lunch Jim said: "Frank, I'll tell you why I wanted to see you. Recently I went down to Skyland, Virginia, on a stag party with a group of friends. We had a great time. We all slept on cots at night in a large, one-room cabin. Well you know what happened the first night. Instead of going right to sleep we started talking back and forth. One by one they fell asleep until, finally, I was the only one left talking. Every time I stopped talking the fellow next to me would say: 'Why,

Jim? Why?'—and like a fool I would go on, and go into more detail, *until he snored*. Then I realized he had been trying to see how long I could talk!"

We both let out a big laugh.

"Right there," Jim went on, "it suddenly occurred to me that here was the way I bought my first life insurance. I don't know whether you realized what you were doing, Frank, but the first time you called on me, I told you that I was going to tell you the same thing I told every other insurance salesman who came to see me: 'I don't believe in life insurance.'

"Instead of launching into a long argument, like other salesmen did, you merely asked 'Why?' As I explained why, you encouraged me to keep on by repeating, 'Why, Mr. Walker?' The more I talked, the more I realized that I was on the wrong side of the argument. Finally I convinced myself that I was wrong. You didn't sell me. I sold myself. But I never knew just how it happened until that night I talked too much down at Skyland.

"Now, Frank, the point of the story is this: Since I got back, I've sat in my office and sold more lumber, right over the telephone, than I ever sold before, just by asking 'Why?' So I wanted to let you know in case you didn't already know how you sold me my first policy."

Jim Walker is one of Philadelphia's most successful lumbermen and a busy man. I have always been grateful to him for taking me aside to make me realize as I never did before the power of this little word "why."

I am amazed that many salesmen are afraid to use it.

I told this story in our lecture courses a few years ago, and had salesmen and others in various fields of activity all over the country tell me how they started using "why" the next day, and how it helped them. Let's just take one example. In Tampa, Florida, a machinery sales agent got up in our school one night and said: "When I heard Mr. Bettger talk about 'why' last night I thought I'd be afraid to use it. But this morning a man walked into our place and priced a large machine. I told him it was $27,000. He said: 'That's too much money for me.' I said: 'Why?' 'Because,' he said, 'it would never pay for itself.' 'Why?' I asked. 'Do you think it would?' he asked frankly. 'Why not? It has been a wonderful investment for everyone who has bought them,' I replied. 'I couldn't afford it,' he said. 'Why?' I asked. Each time he offered an objection, I asked him 'why.' He then elaborated on his reasons. I let him talk. He talked enough to find that his reasons did not add up right, so he bought that machine. It was one of the quickest sales I ever made. But I know I wouldn't have made it if I had given him my usual long-drawn-out sales talk."

Listen to this: The late Milton S. Hershey, who used to push a candy push-cart around the streets and later made millions out of chocolate bars, thought "why" was so important that he dedicated his life to it! Sounds fantastic, doesn't it? Well, here's how it happened. Milton S. Hershey had three failures before he was forty. "Why?" he asked himself. "Why is it that other men succeed and I fail?" Putting himself through a long quiz he narrowed the answer down to one reason: "I was going ahead without having all the facts." From that day until his death at eighty-eight, his whole life was dedicated to the philosophy of asking *"Why?"* If someone said to him: "It can't be done, Mr. Hershey," he'd say, "Why? Why not?" *And he kept on asking why until he had all the reasons.* Then he'd say, "Now one of us has got to get the answer."

Well! isn't that exactly what J. Elliott Hall of New York discovered was wrong with him in selling? He had been trying to go ahead without having all the facts. That's part of the big lesson I learned from him.

In the next chapter, I have used two actual interviews to illustrate how *why* helps me to get the facts. Also, how I use *why* in connection with another common little phrase that produces such surprising results.

12. HOW I FIND THE
HIDDEN OBJECTION

⋺⟫ ⟪⋵

I KEPT a record one time of more than five thousand interviews to try to find out why people bought, or failed to buy. In 62 percent of the cases, the original objection raised against buying was not the *real* reason at all. I found that only 38 percent of the time did the prospect give me the *real* reason for not buying.

Why is that? Why will people—substantial people—perfectly honest in every other way, mislead and misrepresent facts to sales people? That's something it took me a long time to understand.

The late J. Pierpont Morgan, Sr., one of the shrewdest business men in all history, once said: "A man generally has two reasons for doing a thing—one that sounds good, and a *real* one." Keeping those records for several years certainly proved to me the truth of this statement. So I began experimenting to find some way that I might determine whether the reason given was real or merely one that sounded good. Eventually I hit on a simple little phrase that produced surprising results and which has literally been worth thousands of dollars to me. It's a common everyday phrase. That's

why it's good. That phrase is: "In addition to that . . ."
Let me illustrate how I use it.

For several years I had been trying to sell business insurance to a large carpet-manufacturing concern that was owned and managed by three men. Two of them were in favor of the idea but the third was opposed. He was old, and partly deaf. Every time I talked to him about the matter his hearing took a sudden turn for the worse and he couldn't understand a word I said.

While eating breakfast, one morning, I read an announcement in the newspaper of his sudden death.

Naturally, my first thought after reading the announcement was, "Now I've got a sure sale!"

Several days later I phoned the president of the company and made an appointment. I had previously done considerable business with him. When I arrived at the mill and was ushered into his office I noticed that he didn't seem quite so pleasant as usual.

I sat down. He looked at me. I looked at him. Finally he said: "I guess you're up here to talk to us about that business insurance, aren't you?"

I just grinned a big broad grin.

He didn't smile back one bit. "Well," said he, "we're not going to do anything about it."

"Why?" I asked.

"Well, we're just not going to do anything about it."

"Would you mind telling me *why*, Bob?"

"Because," he explained, "we're losing money. We're in the red, and have been all year. To take out that insurance would cost us about eight or ten thousand dollars a year, wouldn't it?"

"Yes," I agreed.

"Well, we've made up our minds," he went on, "not to spend any more money than we absolutely *must* until we see how long this is going to last."

After a few moments of silence I said: "Bob, in addition to that, isn't there something else in the back of your mind? Isn't there some other reason that makes you hesitate to go on with this plan?"

BOB (*a little smile beginning to play around his mouth*). Well, yes, there *is* something else in my mind.

ME. Would you mind telling me what it is?

BOB. It's those two boys of mine. They finished college and are in here working now. They are up in the mill working in overalls every day from eight to five, and they love it! You don't think I'd be fool enough to go into a plan that will sell out my interest in this business if I die, do you? Where would that leave my boys? They could be kicked out—isn't that right?

There it was. The first objection was just one that *sounded* good. Now that I knew the *real* reason I had a chance. I was able to point out that it was even more important for him to do something now. We worked out a plan which included his sons. A plan which made their situation absolutely secure regardless of who died first, and when.

That sale alone was worth $3,860 to me.

Now why did I ask this man that question? Because I doubted his word? No, not at all. His first objection was so logical and real, I had no reason to doubt his word. In fact, I believed it. But years of experience had taught me the odds were two to one that something else was in the picture. My records proved it. So it became habitual with me to ask this question anyhow, just as a routine check-up. I don't recall ever once having anyone resent my asking it.

When the objection given proves to be the *real* reason, what do I do? Let me give an example. I was having lunch one day at the Union League in Philadelphia with two friends of mine, Neale MacNeill, Jr., sales manager of Sandoz Chemical Company, Philadelphia, and Frank R. Davis, Philadelphia real-estate broker. Neale said: "Frank and I have got a real prospect for you. Don Lindsay was talking to us yesterday about buying some insurance. He's making a lot of money, and you ought to be able to sell him about fifty or a hundred thousand, isn't that right, Frank?"

Frank Davis seemed very enthusiastic about the prospect. He advised me to get right out there the next morning, and he said, "Be sure to tell Don that Neale and I sent you."

Ten o'clock the next morning, I walked into Mr. Lindsay's plant at 54th Street and Paschall Avenue, in Philadelphia. He manufactures electric fixtures. I told his secretary that Mr. MacNeill and Mr. Davis sent me out to see Mr. Lindsay.

As I was ushered into his office he was standing in one corner with an expression on his face that reminded me of Jack Dempsey's scowl just before the opening gong.

I waited, but he wasn't talking. So I said: "Mr. Lindsay,

Neale MacNeill and Frank Davis sent me out to see you. They said you are about to buy some life insurance."

"What the */?!* is this?" shouted Lindsay in a voice that must have been heard out on Paschall Avenue. "You're the *fifth* insurance man they've sent out here in two days. Is this what they call a funny joke?"

Well! was I surprised? I would have burst out in a big laugh but this fellow really had fire in his eyes. Finally I said: "What did you say to Neale and Frank that made them think you were going to buy life insurance?"

Still shouting: "I told them that I had never bought any insurance in my life! I don't believe in life insurance!"

"You've been a very successful business man, Mr. Lindsay," I said. "You must have a good reason for not buying life insurance. Would you mind telling me *why?*"

"Sure, I'll tell you why." (His voice toned down quite a bit.) "I've got all the money I need, and if anything happens to me, my wife and daughters will have all the money they need."

I paused as I thought about what he said. Then: "Mr. Lindsay, *in addition to that,* isn't there some other reason why you've never bought life insurance?"

HE. No, that's the only thing. Isn't that a good enough reason?

ME. May I ask you a personal question?

HE. Go ahead.

ME. Do you owe any money?

HE. I don't owe a dollar in the world!

ME. If you did owe considerable money, would you consider buying life insurance to wipe out the loan at your death?

HE. I might.

ME. Has it occurred to you that, if you should die to-night, automatically there will be a big mortgage placed against your estate by Uncle Sam? And, before your wife and daughters could get a cent they would have to raise cash to pay off that mortgage?

Mr. Lindsay bought the first insurance that day he'd ever bought in his life.

The next day, I saw MacNeill and Davis at lunch. When I told them Lindsay had bought I never saw two men look more surprised. For a while, they wouldn't believe it. But when they realized I wasn't joking they seemed to get a great kick out of it.

"In addition to that, isn't there something else in the back of your mind?" often requires a little additional urging for the other person to open up and talk. Let me illustrate with an unusual experience. In Orlando, Florida, one morning a young salesman came to me at the hotel with a serious problem. About two years previously his company, a New York chemical concern, had mysteriously lost their largest account in Florida, and never were able to find out why they had lost it. They tried everything to regain the business. One of their vice-presidents had come down from New York, but even he had failed to get anywhere.

"When I came with the company one year ago," this promising-looking salesman explained, "they impressed on me the importance of going after that business until I got it back.

I've called on these people regularly now for a year, and to me, it looks hopeless."

I asked him several questions about his interviews with them, particularly his recent interviews.

"Just this morning," he said, "I was there again. I talked with the president, Mr. Jones, but it was the same thing. He wouldn't talk. He just sat there, looking bored. After I stopped talking, there was a long silence, and finally I got up in embarrassment and left."

I suggested that he go right back again that afternoon and tell Mr. Jones he just received word from the head office to go back at once. The salesman and I talked over exactly what he was to say. Then I had him repeat it back to me.

Late that afternoon he telephoned me and was so excited he could hardly speak. He said: "May I come right over to see you? I've got an *order* from Mr. Jones! And I believe the whole trouble is being straightened out. Our Atlanta manager is flying down here tonight!"

It seemed incredible. I guess I was almost as excited about it as he was. I said: "Come on right over and tell me all about it."

Here's the interview he related:

"It all seems so simple, I can hardly believe it. As I walked into Mr. Jones's office, he looked up with surprise."

SALESMAN. Mr. Jones, since I saw you this morning, I received word from our head office in New York to see you at once and get all the facts—exactly *why* we lost your business. Our company is sure you must have had a good reason; someone in our organization must have blundered somehow. Won't you please tell me what it was, Mr. Jones?

JONES. I've told you before. I decided to give another concern a trial. They have proved to be perfectly satisfactory and I wouldn't consider changing.

SALESMAN *(after a few moments of silence)*. Mr. Jones, in addition to that, isn't there some other reason? Isn't there something else in the back of your mind?

(No answer.)

SALESMAN. If there is something else, and you tell me what it is, and we can't clear it up, you'll feel better for having given us the chance. If we are able to prove beyond any question of doubt in your mind that it was an unintentional mistake or oversight, you'll feel better for giving us a chance to correct the wrong. Isn't that right, Mr. Jones?

(Same old thing. Mr. Jones just sat there looking out the window. But this time, I kept quiet, and waited him out. It seemed awfully long, but finally he began to talk.)

"Well, if you want to know, your company discontinued a special discount without notifying us. As soon as I discovered it, I cut them off!"

There was the *real* reason.

Here's what happened: That alert young salesman lost no time. He thanked Mr. Jones gratefully for the information, immediately hurried to the nearest public telephone and called the Atlanta office. They got out their records and then called the New York office. Comparison of records proved Mr. Jones had good reason to believe his discount had been discontinued, although it really had not. The

salesman was instructed to return immediately to Jones's
office. By the time he reached there, Jones had been convinced over the phone of the true facts. The Atlanta manager took entire blame for his failure to properly notify Mr.
Jones of a new method of billing on a net basis.

I hesitated a long while before deciding to make this little
formula public. I was afraid it might be regarded as a trick.
And I don't believe in tricks. I can't use them. They don't
work. I've tried them. And I'm glad they failed because
in the long run, I know that tricks are a losing game in any
business. Nothing will take the place of complete honesty,
first, last, and all the time!

SUMMED UP

Remember these wise words of J. Pierpon Morgan: "A man generally has two reasons for doing a thing; one that sounds good, and a *real* one."

The best formula I ever found to draw out the *real* one is built around those two little questions:

"Why?" and "In addition to that . . . ?"

13. THE FORGOTTEN ART THAT IS MAGIC IN SELLING

→⟩⟩ ⟨⟨←

A FEW years ago I made a six months' coast-to-coast lecture tour with Dale Carnegie. We addressed audiences of several hundred people five nights every week—people anxious to improve themselves and their ability to handle and deal with others; persons in varied occupations: stenographers, teachers, executives, homemakers, attorneys, salesmen.

I had never made a lecture tour before, and it proved to be the most exciting adventure of my life. When I returned home, I was eager to do two things: get back to selling again, and, of course, tell everybody about my exciting experience.

The first man I called on was the president of a wholesale and retail milk and dairy products company of Philadelphia. I had previously done considerable business with him. He seemed genuinely happy to see me. As I sat down opposite him at his desk, he offered me a cigarette, and said, "Frank, tell me all about your trip."

"All right, Jim," I replied, "but first, I'm anxious to hear all about you. What have you been doing? How is Mary? And how is your business?"

I listened with eagerness as he talked about his business and his family. Later he got to telling me about a poker party he and his wife had been in the night before. They had played "Red Dog." Well I had never heard of "Red Dog," and by that time I would much rather have told him about my lecture tour and done some bragging about myself. But I laughed with him as he explained how the game is played and how much fun you can get out of it.

He seemed to have a grand time and when I started to leave he said: "Frank, we've been considering insuring the superintendent of our plant. What would $25,000 cost on his life?"

I never *did* get a chance to talk about myself but I left there with a nice order which some other salesman sold, but probably talked himself out of.

This taught me a lesson which I've had to learn: *the importance of being a good listener,* showing the other person you are sincerely interested in what he is saying, giving him all the eager attention and appreciation that he craves and is so hungry for, but seldom gets!

Try looking straight into the face of the next person who speaks to you, with eager, absorbed interest (even if it is your own wife), and see the magic effect it has both on yourself, and the one who is doing the talking.

There is nothing new about this. Cicero said, 2,000 years ago: "There is an art in silence, and there is an eloquence in it too." But listening has become a forgotten art. Good listeners are rare.

A large national organization recently wrote this special message to all its salesmen:

> The next time you go to the movies, notice how actors listen to the talk of the other characters. To be a great actor, it is as necessary to be a masterful listener, as to be an effective talker. The words of the talker are reflected in the face of the listener as in a mirror. He may steal a scene from the talker by the quality of his listening. A famous movie director has said that many actors fail to become stars because they haven't learned the art of creative listening.

Does the art of listening apply only to salesmen and actors? Why isn't it of tremendous importance to all of us, whatever we do? Do you ever sense, when talking to someone, that what you are saying is not making much of an impression? I found many times people heard me all right, but they weren't listening. The effect of my talking was zero, absolute zero, as far as they were concerned. So I said to myself: "The next time you are talking to a man and this happens, stop! Stop right in the middle of a sentence!" Sometimes I stop right in the middle of a word.

I find people regard it as a courtesy. They are never offended. Nine times out of ten they have something on their minds that they would like to say. And if they do, they won't pay any attention to what we're saying anyhow, until they have got in their two cents' worth.

For example, one of our salesmen (whom we'll call Al) took me to interview the late Francis O'Neill, large paper

converter and manufacturer.   Mr. O'Neill started out as a
paper salesman, then went into business for himself and by
hard, steady work, built one of the foremost paper convert-
ing businesses in the country, the Paper Manufacturers
Company of Philadelphia.   He was one of the most highly
regarded men in the paper industry.   He also had the reputation of being a man of few words.

After the usual introduction, Mr. O'Neill invited us to sit
down.   I began talking to him about taxes in relation to his
estate and his business but he never looked up at me.   I
couldn't see his face.   I could only see the top of his head
as he stared down at his desk.   There was no way of knowing whether he was listening to me.   After perhaps three
minutes I stopped right in the middle of a sentence!   There
followed a seemingly embarrassing silence.   I settled comfortably back in my chair and waited.

About a minute of this was too much for Al.   He began
squirming nervously in his chair; he was afraid my nerve
had failed me in the presence of this important man.   He
must save the situation.   So he began to talk.   If I could
have reached him under the table, I would have kicked him
in the shins!   Watching closely until he looked over my way,
I shook my head for him to stop.   Luckily Al caught the
signal and stopped instantly.

Then followed more awkward silence, fully another minute.   (It seemed much longer.)   Finally raising his head
slightly, the paper products manufacturer glanced up.   He
could see that I was entirely relaxed, and obviously waiting
for him to say something.

We looked at each other in an expectant manner. (Al told me afterward that he never saw anything like it. He couldn't understand what was going on.) Finally Mr. O'Neill broke the silence. I have found that if you wait long enough, the other fellow will *always* break the silence. Usually he was a man of few words but he talked earnestly now for half an hour. As long as he was willing to talk, I encouraged him to go on.

When he finished, I said: "Mr. O'Neill, you have given me some important information. I can see you have given this subject far more thought than most business men. You have been a very successful man, and I wouldn't be egotistical enough to think that I could come in here, and, in a few minutes give you the right solution to the problem which you have spent two years trying to solve. However I'd like to take some time to give it further study. I may be able to come back with some ideas that will be helpful."

What in the beginning looked like a most unsatisfactory interview, terminated very successfully. Why? Simply because I got this man to talk about his problems. As I listened, he gave me valuable clues as to his needs. A few tactful questions enabled me to obtain the key to his whole situation, and what he wanted to accomplish. This case subsequently developed into a large line of business.

All of us would profit by uttering this prayer every morning: "Oh Lord, help me to keep my big mouth shut, until I know what I am talking about . . . Amen."

There were many times when I could have kicked myself in the teeth for talking on and on, when I should have been able to see the man wasn't listening, but my mind was so intent on what I was saying that it took too long for me to get it through my thick head that he wasn't paying attention.

Many times there is a parade of thoughts passing across the mind of a man, and unless we give him a chance to do some of the talking, we have no way of knowing what he is thinking.

Experience has taught me that it is a good rule to make sure the other fellow does a liberal share of the talking in the first half. Then when I talk I am more sure of the facts and more likely to have an attentive listener.

We all hate to be outsmarted, outwitted, interrupted, cut off before we finish, by some flannel-mouth who knows what we are going to say before we say it. You know the kind; he throws his mouth into high gear before his brain is turning over, explains to you where and why you are mistaken, and straightens you out before you can make yourself clear. By that time, you feel like straightening *him* out—with a left and right uppercut to the chin!

Even if he *is* right, you hate to admit it, and if he's a salesman, you'll sometimes resort to a lie to get rid of this smart guy, then go two miles out of your way to buy the same thing, even if you have to pay more.

As a young man, Benjamin Franklin was cocksure and wanted to do most of the talking, telling people where they were wrong until they crossed on the other side of the street to avoid him. A Quaker friend kindly informed him of this unpardonable fault, and convinced Ben by mentioning several instances. Over half a century later, when he was seventy-nine years old, Franklin wrote these words in his famous autobiography:

> Considering that in conversation knowledge was obtained rather by the use of the ears than of the *tongue*, I gave *Silence second place* among the virtues I determined to cultivate.

How about you? Do you ever catch yourself thinking about what you're going to say, rather than listening attentively? I found that when I wasn't listening to a man attentively, I got my facts confused, lost track of the main issue, and frequently came to wrong conclusions!

Yes, it is quite true that there are times when people are so flattered by our undivided attention and eagerness to hear what they have to say, that they go overboard and give us a long "workout." For instance, one of our salesmen arranged to take me to interview George J. DeArmond, prominent wholesale upholstery goods and cabinet hardware merchant, 925 Filbert Street, Philadelphia. The appointment was at 11 A.M. Six hours later, John and I staggered out of this merchant's office and dove into a coffee shop to relieve our aching heads. It was plain to see that John was disappointed with my sales talk. It would be exaggeration to say that it lasted five minutes.

The second appointment, we made certain, was set for *after* lunch. This "conference" began at two o'clock, and if our prospect's chauffeur hadn't come to our rescue at 6 P.M., we might be there yet!

Later, we figured up that there had been a total of half an hour's actual selling talk, and over nine hours of listening to this old fellow's thrilling story of his business life. And it *was* thrilling and inspiring as he told how he started with nothing, built up, went through depressions, had a nervous breakdown at fifty, formed a partnership only to have his partner go bad, and how he finally laid the foundation for one of the finest wholesale merchandising businesses in the East. It had probably been years since anyone was willing to listen long enough for this man to tell his story in full. He was *starved* for just such an opportunity. He became excited, and at times his eyes filled up from emotion.

Evidently, most people were giving this man their tongue, instead of their ears. We simply reversed this process, and were handsomely rewarded. We insured his fifty-year-old son, J. Keyser DeArmond, for $100,000 for the protection of his business.

Dr. Joseph Fort Newton, famous preacher, author, and newspaper columnist, told me: "Salesmen need to listen, and so do preachers. One of my principal duties is listening in on human lives."

"Not long ago," Dr. Newton said, "a woman sat across my desk talking rapidly. She was almost stone deaf and could hardly hear a word I said. The story she told was pitiful, heartbreaking, and she told it in minute detail. Seldom had I listened to a sadder history as she poured out her pent-up heartache.

" 'You have helped me so much,' she said at last. 'I just had to tell somebody, and you were kind enough to listen and give me sympathy.'

"Yet I had said hardly a word," related Dr. Newton, "and I doubt whether she heard what I said. Anyway I shared her loneliness and sorrow, and that helped to lift the load. She gave me the sweetest smile as she left."

Dorothy Dix, one of the most widely read newspaper columnists in the world, was right when she wrote: "The shortcut to popularity is to lend everyone your ears, instead of giving them your tongue. There is nothing you can possibly say to an individual that would be half as interesting to him as the things he is dying to tell you about himself. And all you need, in order to get the reputation of being a fascinating companion, is to say: 'How wonderful! Do tell me some more.'"

I no longer worry about being a brilliant conversationalist. I simply try to be a good listener. I notice that people who do that are usually welcome wherever they go.

SUMMARY

PART TWO

POCKET REMINDERS

1. The most important secret of salesmanship is to find out what the other fellow wants, then help him find the best way to get it.

2. If you want to hit the bull's-eye, remember the sage advice of Dale Carnegie: "There is only one way under high heaven to get anybody to do anything. Just one way. And that is by making the other person want to do it. Remember, there is no other way."
   When you show a man what he wants, he will move heaven and earth to get it.

3. Cultivate the art of asking questions. Questions, rather than positive statements, can be the most effective means of making a sale, or winning people to your way of thinking. Inquire rather than attack.

4. Find the key issue, the most vulnerable point, then stick to it.

5. Learn how to use the most important word in selling, that powerful little one-word question, "Why?" Remember that Milton S. Hershey, who failed three times before he was forty, thought this word was so important in business that he dedicated his life to it.

6. To find the hidden objection, the *real* reason, remember what J. Pierpont Morgan said: "A man generally has two reasons for doing a thing—one that sounds good, and a *real* one." It is probably two to one that something else is in the picture. Ask those two little questions: "Why?" and "In addition to that . . . ?" Try using them for one week. You will be surprised with your results in overcoming objections.

7. Remember the forgotten art that is magic in selling. Be a good listener. Show the other person you are sincerely interested in what he is saying, give him all the eager attention and appreciation that everyone craves and is so hungry for, but seldom gets. It is one of the most important principles of the formula for success in selling. Yes, it *is* magic in selling!

Part Three

SIX WAYS TO WIN AND HOLD
THE CONFIDENCE OF OTHERS

14.

THE BIGGEST LESSON I EVER LEARNED ABOUT CREATING CONFIDENCE

→≫ ≪←

WHEN I started out to sell, I had the good fortune to be placed under the supervision of Karl Collings, who for forty years was among the leading salesmen of his company.

Mr. Collings' biggest asset was his remarkable ability to inspire the confidence of others. As soon as he began to talk, you felt, "Here is a man I can trust; he knows his business, and he's dependable." I noticed this the first time I met him. One day I learned why.

A promising prospect had told me to "Come back after the first of the month. I might do something," but I was afraid to go back. In fact, I was so discouraged about that time, each day I was thinking of quitting. So I asked Mr. Collings if he would go with me to see this man. He gave that double take look at my "droopy puss" and said: "Sure, I'll go."

Well, he made the sale with surprising ease. Boy, was I excited! I figured up my commission. It would be $259—and me dodging bill collectors! But a few days later I got the bad news. Due to a physical impairment, the contract was issued "modified."

111

"Must we tell the man it isn't standard?" I pleaded. "He won't know it, unless you tell him, will he?"

"No, but *I'll* know it. And *you'll* know it," answered Mr. Collings quietly.

Soon we were sitting across the desk from the prospective buyer.

Mr. Collings began: "I could tell you this policy is standard and you probably would never know the difference, but it's not." Then he showed the man the difference. "However," continued Collings, looking our man straight in the eye, "I believe this contract gives you the protection you need and I would like you to give it very serious consideration."

Without the slightest hesitation the man said, "I'll take it," and immediately wrote his check for the full year's payment.

Watching Karl Collings in that interview showed me *why* people believed him, why they so readily gave him their complete confidence. That interview helped me more than all the preaching he might ever have done. He deserved confidence! It showed in his eyes.

"No—but *I'll* know it," proved to be the key to Karl's true character. The deep meaning behind those simple words of his, I've never been able to forget. My greatest source of courage, whenever things have looked dark, has come from believing in the wisdom of this philosophy: Not—Will the *other person* believe it. The real test is, do *you* believe it?

Once I carried the following clipping in my pocket and read it until it became a part of me:

The wisest and best salesman is always the one

who bluntly tells the truth about his article. He looks his prospective customer in the eye and tells his story. That is always impressive. And if he does not sell the first time, he leaves a trail of trust behind. A customer, as a rule, cannot be fooled a second time by some shady or clever talk that does not square with the truth. Not the best talker wins the sale—but the most honest talker . . . there is something in the look of the eye, the arrangement of words, the spirit of a salesman that immediately compels trust or distrust . . . being bluntly honest is always safe and best.

—George Matthew Adams

I am not a C.L.U. (Chartered Life Underwriter), but I have tried to follow their code. Any salesman would profit by adopting it: "In all my relations with clients, I agree to observe the following rule of professional conduct: I shall, in the light of all the circumstances surrounding my client, which I shall make every effort to ascertain and understand, give him that service which, had I been in the same circumstances, I would have applied to myself."

To win and hold the confidence of others, Rule One is:

DESERVE CONFIDENCE

15. A VALUABLE LESSON I LEARNED ABOUT CREATING CONFIDENCE FROM A GREAT PHYSICIAN

⊟≫ ≪⊟

I ARRIVED in Dallas, Texas, one Saturday evening a few years ago with a streptococcus infection in my throat. I couldn't speak. And I was scheduled for a series of lectures for five nights opening on Monday night! A doctor was called in. He gave me a treatment, but the next morning my condition was worse. It seemed impossible for me to go on with the lectures.

Then I was referred to Dr. O. M. Marchman, 814 Medical Arts Building, in Dallas. He came in and performed what the first doctor said would be *im*possible. I was able to go on the platform every night and deliver *all* my talks!

During a treatment one morning Dr. Marchman asked me where I made my home. When I told him Philadelphia his eyes lighted up. "Is that so? You come from the medical center of the world," he said. "I spend six weeks each summer in your home town attending lectures and clinics."

Well, was I surprised! Here was a man enjoying one of the largest practices in the Southwest, yet at sixty-six years of age he was so interested in keeping abreast of the latest scientific developments in his profession that he spent his six weeks' vacation each year attending lectures and clinics. Is it any wonder a man like that was regarded as the outstanding ear, nose, and throat specialist in Dallas, Texas?

Frank Taylor, purchasing agent of General Motors many years ago, said: "I like to do business with the fellow who informs himself about his own business, who can tell exactly what he has that I can use, and goes at his work without wasting my time or his. I like the man with useful ideas, the man who can show me how to get more goods or better goods for the same amount of money. He helps me handle my job to the satisfaction of my employers. I try to favor any salesman who is absolutely honest about his goods, and who sees their limitations as well as their virtues. I have never had a misunderstanding with such a man."

Back in the days when I was struggling to get ahead, there were sixteen salesmen working out of our office in Philadelphia. Two of them were producing about seventy per cent of the business. I noticed that these two men were continually being consulted by the other salesmen. I probably took advantage of their generosity more than anybody. Finally, it struck me as being very significant that these leaders were the best informed. One time I asked one of them where he got all his information. He said: "I subscribe to services that give all the legal answers, sales ideas, etc., and I read the best journals and magazines."

"Where do you get the time to read and study all these things?" I asked.

"I take the time!" he replied.

That made me feel guilty. I thought: "If he can take

the time, I can too. His time is worth ten times as much as mine." So I subscribed to one of the services he recommended, paying the cost monthly. It wasn't too long afterward that I closed a nice sale which I never would have even seen if I hadn't started that course. Naturally I was enthusiastic about it, and I told one of our other men in the office. I urged him to take the course too. But he said: "I can't afford it now."

The next day, as I started to cross Broad Street at an intersection, I was nearly knocked down by a handsome, high-powered car. As I looked up, I recognized the owner. It was the man who told me the day before that he *couldn't afford* the $48 service. Later that man couldn't afford his car, either!

I have traveled all over the country attending sales meetings and clinics. At those meetings, I've always noticed that the leaders are men who know their business.

Billy Rose, in his column "Pitching Horseshoes," wrote not very long ago: "This is the age of the specialist. Charm and good manners are worth up to $30 a week. After that, the pay-off is in direct ratio to the amount of specialized know-how in a fellow's head."

How long should we keep on studying and learning? Well, Dr. Marchman of Dallas, Texas, was still going strong at sixty-six, and he didn't think there *ever* was a good time to stop. Henry Ford said: "Anyone who stops learning is old—whether at twenty or eighty. Anyone who keeps learning stays young. The greatest thing in life is to keep your mind young."

So if you want to have confidence in yourself, and win and hold the confidence of others, I find it an essential rule to:

KNOW YOUR BUSINESS
AND KEEP ON KNOWING YOUR BUSINESS.

16. THE QUICKEST WAY I EVER DISCOVERED TO WIN CONFIDENCE

➤➤➤ ≪≪≪

THE *quickest* way that I ever discovered to win the confidence of others is to—well, let me illustrate with an actual interview. The scene of this interview was in the office of the late A. Conrad Jones, treasurer of the I. P. Thomas Company, Camden, N. J., large fertilizer manufacturers. Mr. Jones didn't know me and I quickly found out that he knew practically nothing about my company.

Let's listen in on what happened as the interview proceeded:

ME. Mr. Jones, what companies are you insured in?
JONES. The New York Life, Metropolitan, and Provident
ME. Well, you've picked the best!
JONES (*obviously pleased*). Do you think so?
ME. None better in the world!
(*Then I proceeded to tell him some facts about his companies, things that definitely established them as great institutions. For example, I told him that the Metropolitan was the largest corporation in the world; an amazing organization that in some communities had insured every man, woman, and child.*)

Was he bored? No sir! He listened eagerly as I told him some things about his companies that he apparently had never heard before. I could see that he felt proud for having used such excellent judgment, investing his money with these great companies.

Did this honest praise of my competitors hurt me? Well, let's see what happened:

As I made these brief but favorable comments, I closed by saying: "You know, Mr. Jones, we have *three* great companies right here in Philadelphia: the Provident, Fidelity, and Penn Mutual. They stand among the major companies of the country."

He seemed impressed with my knowledge of my competitors, and my going out of my way to praise them. When I placed my own company in the same class with other companies with which he already was familiar, he was better prepared to accept my statements as being accurate.

Here's what happened: I insured A. Conrad Jones personally and within a few months his firm bought from me a large line of business insurance on the lives of its four top executives. When the president, Henry R. Lippincott, questioned me about the Fidelity, the company where all this insurance was to be placed, Mr. Jones broke in and repeated almost verbatim what I had told him months before about "the three great Philadelphia companies."

No—praising my competitors did not make those sales, but it did get me on first base, which later placed me in a position to go to bat with the bases full! Then luck was with me, and I connected for a homer.

With me a quarter of a century of praising competitors has proved to be a very happy and profitable way of doing business. All through life in our daily contacts, socially and in business, aren't we all trying to win the confidence of each other? I've found that one of the quickest ways to win and hold the confidence of others is to apply the rule spoken by one of the world's greatest diplomats, Benjamin Franklin: "I will speak ill of no man—and speak all the good I know of everybody."

So, Rule Three is:

PRAISE YOUR COMPETITORS

17.

♦

HOW TO GET
KICKED OUT!

→⇛ ⬱←

I WAS being granted the courtesy of a final interview by
Arthur C. Emlen, president of Harrison, Mertz & Emlen,
prominent landscape architects and engineers, 5220
Greene Street, Germantown, Philadelphia. It involved a
rather large line of business, and was competitive. Mr.
Emlen called the other four members of the firm into his
office. As we all sat down, I sensed somehow that I was
about to get the brushoff. And I was right.

Here's the interview:

EMLEN. Mr. Bettger, I haven't got very good news for
you. We've given this matter very careful study and have
decided to place the business through another broker.

ME. Would you mind telling me why?

EMLEN. Well, he presented the same proposition as you,
but his cost is much less.

ME. May I see the figures?

EMLEN. That would hardly be fair to the other broker
would it?

ME. Did he see *my* proposal?

121

EMLEN. Ah . . . mmn yes, but only because we wanted him to give us figures on the same plan.

ME. Why not give me the same privilege you gave him? How can you lose?

EMLEN (*looking around at his associates*). What do you think, men?

MERTZ. O.K. What have we got to lose?

(*Emlen handed me the proposal. As soon as I looked at it, I knew something was wrong. It was more than exaggeration. It was misrepresentation!*)

ME. May I use your telephone?

EMLEN (*a little surprised*). Go ahead.

ME. Can you listen in on your extension, Mr. Emlen?

EMLEN. Sure.

(*We were soon connected with the local manager of the company whose figures the other broker submitted.*)

ME. Hello, Gil! This is Frank Bettger. I'd like to get some rates from you. Have you got your rate-book handy?

GIL. Yes, Frank. Go right ahead.

ME. Look for age forty-six on that new "Modified Life Plan" of yours. What is the rate?

(*Gil gave me the rate and it compared exactly with the figures on the proposal in my hand. Forty-six was Mr. Emlen's age.*)

ME. What is the first dividend?

(*Gil read it off to me and that also checked correctly.*)

ME. Now, Gil, will you give me the first twenty years' dividend scale?

GIL. I can't do that, Frank, we've only got *two* dividends we can quote.

ME. Why?

GIL. Well, this is a new contract, and the company doesn't know what their experience will be.

ME. Can't you estimate it?

GIL. No, Frank, we can't accurately foretell future conditions. Therefore, the law doesn't permit estimates of future dividends.

(*The proposal I held in my hand displayed an extremely liberal estimate for dividends for twenty years.*)

ME. Thank you, Gil. I hope I'll have some more business for you soon.

Mr. Emlen had listened in on the whole conversation. As we hung up there was a short pause. I just sat quietly looking at him. Raising his eyes he looked at me, then at his partners, and said, "Well, that's that!"

The business was mine without another question. I believe my competitor would have had it, if he had simply told the truth! He not only lost that sale; he lost all chance of ever doing business with these men again. In addition to that, he lost his own self-respect.

How do I know? Because several years before, I had lost out in exactly the same set of circumstances. Only then *I* was on the wrong side. I was in competition with a friend of mine. If I had merely presented the facts, I probably would have got the order, or at least half of it, because the president of the firm I was trying to sell wanted to give me the business. It would have meant a lot to me at that time. The temptation was too great and I exaggerated the possibilities of what I was selling. It really was misrepresentation. Well somebody became suspicious and checked up with my company. I lost the business; I lost the confidence and respect of my good friend; I lost the respect of my competitor; and worst of all, I lost my own self-respect.

It was a bitter experience. I was so shocked at my blunder that I thought of it all that night. I was years recovering from the humiliation of it. But I am *glad* I lost, because it taught me that Karl Collings' philosophy: "Yes, but *I'll* know it" was the best after all. I made up my mind: I shall never again want anything I'm not entitled to; it costs too much!

18. I FOUND THIS AN INFALLIBLE WAY TO GAIN A MAN'S CONFIDENCE

→》》 《《←

I'VE been told that probably the most important thing a trial lawyer does in pleading a case before court is to bring on his witnesses. Naturally the judge and jury feel that the lawyer is prejudiced in his views so they are likely to discount some of the things he says. But good testimony from a reliable witness exerts a powerful influence on the court in establishing confidence for the lawyer as he builds his case.

Let's see how witnesses can help in selling.

For many years upon delivery of each contract I sold, the buyer signed our company's printed "acceptance receipt." I had these receipts photostated and pasted on sheets of paper in a loose-leaf book. I found they exerted a powerful influence in establishing confidence for me among strangers. Coming toward the "close," I usually say something like this: "Mr. Allen, naturally, I am prejudiced. Anything I say about this plan would be favorable; so I want you to talk with someone who has no interest in selling it. May I use your telephone for a minute?" Then I call one of my "witnesses" on the phone—preferably someone whose name the prospect

125

recognized as he glanced over the signatures on the "acceptance receipts." Often, it is a neighbor or friend. Sometimes it is an out-of-town call. Long distance calls, I find most effective. (Now remember! I make this call on my prospect's phone. But I immediately ask the operator to report the cost of the call, and *I always pay it immediately.*)

When I first tried this, I was afraid the prospect would stop me, but none ever has. In fact, they seem pleased to talk with my "witness." Sometimes it is an old friend, and the conversation drifts into channels far removed from the original purpose of the call.

I stumbled across this idea quite by accident, but have found it a superb way to bring on your witnesses. I never had much success overcoming objections with clever comebacks. They read well in textbooks, but when I tried to use them, they only seemed to lead into an argument. I found it a hundred times more effective when I could get a direct testimony from one of my "witnesses," and they are as close as the telephone.

How do my witnesses feel about this? They always seem glad to give advice. When I go to see them to express my appreciation, I find it has had a double-barreled effect, for in their effort to sell my new prospect, they have become more enthusiastic about what I have sold them.

Years ago a close friend of mine was in the market for an oil burner for his home. He received letters and catalogues from various companies. One of these letters read something like this: "Here's a list of your neighbors who heat their homes with our burner. Why don't you just step over to the phone and call up Mr. Jones, your neighbor, and ask him how he likes our heater?"

My friend *did* pick up the phone and talk to some of his neighbors on that list. And he *did* buy that heater. Although this happened eighteen years ago, my friend said recently: "I have always remembered the wording of that letter."

Several weeks after I gave a school in Tulsa, Oklahoma, a salesman wrote and told me how he began using this idea with sensational effect in his approach. Here it is:

"Mr. Harris, there is a store over in Oklahoma City about the same size as yours, that secured over forty new customers last month because they began selling a certain nationally advertised article. If it were possible for you to talk to the owner of that store, wouldn't you want to ask him some questions about it."

"Yes!"

"May I use your telephone for a minute?"

"Sure, go right ahead."

"I immediately called the owner of that store on the phone and then let the two merchants talk," wrote this salesman. "I have found this not only a perfect approach," he continued, "but one of the best selling ideas I have ever used."

Let me give you just one more experience which Dale Carnegie told me about. I'll let Dale tell it himself:

"I wanted to know where I could go in Canada, to a new camp, where I could depend on good food, good beds, good fishing and hunting. So I wrote to the recreation department of New Brunswick. Shortly afterward, I got answers from thirty or forty camps, literature of all sorts with them, which confused me more than ever.   But one man sent me a letter and said, "Why don't you call up these people in New York City who have been to our camp recently and ask them about it?'

"I recognized the name of one man on the list, and called him up.   He went into eulogies telling how wonderful the camp was. . . . There was one man whom I knew, and whom I could believe, and who would tell me what I wanted to know. *A direct testimony.* I could get confidential information.   None of the others produced *witnesses.*   Surely all these other camps had them, but didn't bother to use the one thing that would gain my confidence more quickly than any other!"

So an infallible way to gain a man's confidence quickly is to:

BRING ON YOUR WITNESSES

19. ♦ HOW TO LOOK YOUR BEST

-》》》 《《《-

HERE is an idea which was given to me thirty years ago and I have been using it ever since. One of the most successful men in our organization said to me: "Want to know something? Every once in a while when I look at you I have to laugh. Most of the time you dress like a freak!" Well, that was pretty hard to take, but this old fellow was one of those "forty-minute eggs." I knew he was sincere, so I listened.

Then he let me have it—*and good.* "You let your hair grow so long, you look like an old-time football player. Why don't you get your hair cut like a business man? Have it trimmed every week, so that it will always look the same. You don't know how to tie your tie. Go take lessons from a good haberdasher. Your color combinations are positively funny! Why don't you put yourself in the hands of an expert? He'll teach you how to dress."

"I can't afford anything like that," I protested.

"What do you mean you can't afford anything like that?" he snapped back. "It won't cost you a cent. In fact, it will save you money. Now listen to me. Pick out a good haberdasher. If you don't know anyone go over and see Joe Scott, of Scott and Hunsicker. Tell him I sent you. Tell him frankly that you don't have much money to spend on clothes, but you want to know how to be well dressed. Tell him that if he will advise you and teach you, whatever money you have to spend on clothes you will spend with him right in *his* store. He'll like that. He'll take a personal interest in you; show you what you should wear. He'll save you time and money. And you'll make more money, because people will have more confidence in you."

Such an idea would never have occurred to me. That was the best advice I ever heard on how to be well dressed. I've always been glad I listened.

I placed myself in the hands of a good barber named Ruby Day. I told him I was coming to him every week; that I wanted him to cut my hair to look like a business man, and keep it trimmed to look the same all the time. This cost me more money than I ever spent before in a barbershop, but I *saved* money on the next step.

I went to Joe Scott and he gladly agreed to the deal. He gave me lessons in how to tie my tie; stood alongside of me while I practiced, until I got the knack almost as well as he. Whenever I bought a suit of clothes, he took a live interest, then helped me choose shirts, ties, and socks to match the suit. He told me the kind of hat to wear with it, helped me pick out the proper topcoat. From time to time he gave me little talks on how to be well dressed. He gave me a booklet to read that helped me. Another important bit of advice he gave me saved me enough money over the years to pay for several suits of clothes. I was in the habit of wearing the same suit until it looked as though I'd slept in it. Then I'd send it to the tailor's to be cleaned and pressed. "Frequent pressing," Joe Scott explained, "takes the animal life out of the cloth, and the suit wears out much quicker. Nobody should wear the same suit two days in succession. If you only have two suits, alternate each day. After each wearing, your coat and vest should be hung on a hanger, your trousers hung straight, *not* over the hanger's cross-bar. If you do this, the creases will disappear and your clothes will rarely need pressing, until you send them to the dry cleaners."

Later, after I could afford it, Joe proved to me that it is a great economy to invest in several suits. That enabled me to let each suit hang several days after wearing.

My friend, George Geuting, a real shoe man, told me that these same rules apply to wearing shoes. "If you alternate pairs every day," George said, "shoes feel better, hold their life and shape better, and last much longer."

Someone has said: "Clothes don't make the man, but they do make ninety per cent of what you see of him." Unless a man looks the part, people won't believe what he says is important. And there is no doubt about it; when you feel well dressed, it improves your mental attitude toward yourself, and gives you more self-confidence.

So here's the most practical idea I ever heard on how to improve your appearance: "Put yourself in the hands of an expert."

LOOK YOUR BEST

SUMMARY

PART THREE

POCKET REMINDERS

1. Deserve Confidence. The real test is: do you believe it, *not,* will the other person believe it?

2. To have confidence in yourself, and win and hold the confidence of others, an essential rule is to:
   Know your business . . . and keep on knowing your business!

3. One of the quickest ways to win and hold the confidence of others is to apply the rule of one of the world's greatest diplomats, Benjamin Franklin: "I will speak ill of no man—and speak all the good I know of everybody." Praise Your Competitors!

4. Cultivate the habit of making understatements; never exaggerate! Remember Karl Collings' philosophy: "Yes, but *I'll* know it."

5. An infallible way to gain a man's confidence quickly is to:
Bring on your witnesses. And they are as close as the telephone.

6. Look Your Best. "Put yourself in the hands of an expert."

Part Four

HOW TO MAKE PEOPLE WANT
TO DO BUSINESS WITH YOU

❧ ❧

20. AN IDEA I LEARNED FROM LINCOLN HELPED ME MAKE FRIENDS

⊷⟫⟫⟫ ⟨⟨⟨⊶

ONE DAY, as I was leaving the office of a young attorney, I made a remark which caused him to look up at me in surprise. It was my first call on him, and I had failed to interest him the slightest bit in what I was trying to sell. But what I said as I started to leave interested him immensely.

Here is all I said: "Mr. Barnes, I believe you've got a great future ahead of you. I'll never annoy you, but if you don't mind I'm going to keep in touch with you from time to time."

"What do you mean, I've got a great future?" asked the young lawyer. I knew by the way he spoke he thought I was just handing him some cheap flattery.

I said: "I heard you speak a couple of weeks ago at the Seigel Home-Town Association Meeting, and I thought you made one of the finest speeches I have ever heard. That wasn't only my opinion. I wish you could have heard some of the fine things I heard our members say after you left."

Was he pleased? He seemed thrilled! I asked him how he happened to get started speaking in public. He talked for some time, and when I left, he said: "Come in and see me any time, Mr. Bettger."

Over a period of years that man built a large law practice. In fact, he became one of the most successful lawyers in the city. I kept in close touch with him, and as he grew and prospered, I was able to do more and more business with him. We became good friends, and he was one of my best centers of influence.

Finally he became counsel for such companies as the Pennsylvania Sugar Refining Company; Midvale (steel) Company; and Horn & Hardart (baking) Company. He was elected to the board of directors of some of these companies. Later he retired from active practice and accepted one of the highest honors a man can have bestowed on him by his state; he became Justice of the Supreme Court of the State of Pennsylvania. His name was H. Edgar Barnes.

I never did stop telling Edgar Barnes how much I believed in him. Frequently he told me confidentially of his progress. I shared his happiness with him and more than once I said: "I always knew you were going to be one of the leading lawyers of Philadelphia." Justice Barnes never mentioned it to me directly, but remarks made by mutual friends gave me the feeling that the encouragement I gave him along the way had just a little bit to do with his remarkable success.

Do men like you to show that you believe in them and expect bigger things of them? If your interest is sincere, I don't know of anything they appreciate more. We hear a lot about the starving people of Europe and China, but there are millions of people starving right here in America. Thousands of people right in your city and my city are hungry—hungry for honest praise and appreciation!

Abraham Lincoln wrote something many years ago about winning friends. It is old, but it has helped me so much that I am going to repeat it here:

> If you would win a man to your cause, first convince him that you are his sincere friend. Therein is a drop of honey that catches his heart, which is the high road to his reason, and which, when once gained, you will find but little trouble in convincing his judgment of the justice of your cause, if indeed that cause be a just one.

Years ago I was referred to a young clerk working in the Girard Trust Company, Broad and Chestnut Streets, Philadelphia. He was then twenty-one years of age. I managed to make a small sale to him. One day after I got to know him better, I said: "Clint, some day you're going to be president of the Girard Trust Company, or one of its high officers." He laughed at me, but I insisted: "No, I'm serious. Why shouldn't you? What's going to stop you? You've got all the natural qualifications. You're young, ambitious, make an excellent appearance. You're got a grand personality. Remember all the officers of this bank were just clerks at one time. Some day, they will pass on or retire. Somebody will take their place. Why shouldn't you be one? You'll do it if you want to!"

I urged him to take an advanced course in banking, and a course in public speaking. He took those courses. Then one day the employees were called into a meeting and one of the officers told them about a problem confronting the bank. He said the officers wanted the benefit of any suggestions from the employees.

My young friend, Clinton Stiefel, got up at that meeting and gave them his ideas on the problem. He put his talk across with so much confidence and enthusiasm, it surprised everybody. Friends gathered around him after the meeting and congratulated him and said they were amazed he could speak so well.

The next day the officer who had conducted the meeting called Clint into his office, paid him a high compliment, and said the bank was going to adopt one of his suggestions.

It wasn't long afterward that Clint Stiefel was made head of a department. Where is he today? Clinton S. Stiefel is vice-president of the Provident Trust Company, one of the oldest and finest banking institutions in Pennsylvania.

Mr. Stiefel goes out of his way to recommend me to others and when he has bought insurance personally from time to time, I haven't had to worry about competition.

Many years ago I went to see two friends of mine, promising young business men, but they seemed to be depressed. So I gave them a pep talk. I told them of the fine things I often heard about them in the trade, from big concerns, long-established businesses—their competitors! I reminded them of their small beginning in one room only five years before. I asked them this question: "How did you ever get started in this business?" This got them both laughing and talking about their early hardships. Some I'd never heard before. I told them I didn't know of anybody in their line of business who had a more brilliant outlook for the future than they had. It seemed to revive their spirits to hear that they were now regarded by their competitors as being among the leaders in their industry. They probably knew this, but evidently no one had given them any praise for so long that it was just what the doctor ordered!

When I left the younger of the two men walked out to the elevator with me, his arm over my shoulder. As I stepped on the elevator, he laughed and said: "Come in *every* Monday morning, Frank, and give us a pep talk, will you?"

I did go back there many times over the years and give them pep talks, including talks about what I had to sell. These men continued to grow and prosper, and the business I did with them grew too.

I have been inspired by reading about a few great men in history, but my biggest inspiration, and some of the best ideas I've ever learned, have come from the men I have done business with, and friends I have made. As I profited by their ideas, I have made it a point to tell them about it. I find that people love to hear that they have helped you. Let me give you just one example:

I was talking one day with Morgan H. Thomas, then sales manager of the Garrett-Buchanan Paper Company, 116 South Sixth Street, Philadelphia. I said: "Morgan, you have been a great inspiration to me. You have helped me make more money and enjoy better health."

Did he believe me? He said: "What are you trying to do, kid me?" "No," I said, "I mean exactly what I said. A few years ago your president, Mr. Sinex, told me that you came to work here when you were just a boy and you had to get in at seven o'clock in the morning and sweep the place out before anyone else arrived. 'Now,' he said, 'Morgan is sales manager, but he still gets in at seven o'clock in the morning. He is still the first man in this place every morning!'

"Well, I thought, to get in here at seven o'clock, means that Morgan Thomas must get up not later than *six*. And if he can get up at six o'clock in the morning and look as well as he does, I'm going to try it. So I did. I joined the six o'clock club, Morgan, and I feel better than I've ever felt in my life, and I get so much more done. You have helped me make more money." I know Mr. Thomas was happy to hear me say he had helped me.

Today Morgan Thomas is president of the Garrett-Buchanan Paper Company, second largest distributors of paper products in the United States. Morgan is one of my biggest clients and I have sold most of the key men in that fine organization.

Here is a question I have used countless times: "How did you ever get started in this business, Mr. Roth?"

A man will generally answer: "Well, that's a long story." When a man begins to open up and talk about his own business, I am always fascinated to hear how he got started; his small beginning; his many difficulties; how he overcame them. It is a great romance to me. It is a greater romance to him. He rarely finds anyone interested enough to want to hear all about it. He loves to tell his story if you encourage him. If you are really interested, and seem to be benefiting by his experiences, he'll sometimes go into great detail.

After I leave him I make notes of many of these things: where he was born, his wife's name, names of his children, his ambitions, and hobbies. I have these records on cards in my files dating back twenty-five years.

Sometimes men are astonished that I remember so much about them. Being really interested in people has been of great help to me in opening up many warm and lasting friendships.

There seems to be something magic in this question: "How did you ever get started in this business?" It has frequently helped me get favorable interviews with hardboiled prospects who were too busy to see me. Let's just take one typical experience. Here is an actual interview with a busy wood tank manufacturer who apparently had only one thought in his mind about salesmen: Get rid of them.

ME. Mr. Roth, good morning! My name is Bettger of the Fidelity Mutual Life Insurance Company. Do you know Mr. Walker, Jim Walker? *(handing card of introduction to him with a personal notation from Jim Walker).*

ROTH *(looking very disagreeable . . . glances at card . . . tosses it on desk and says angrily).* Are you another salesman?

ME. Yes, but . . .

ROTH *(breaking in before I can say another word).* You're the tenth salesman who's been in here today. I've got too

many important things to do. I can't be listening to salesmen all day. Don't bother me, see! I haven't got the time!

ME. I've stopped for just a moment, to introduce myself
to you, Mr. Roth. The purpose of my call is to make an
appointment with you for tomorrow, or later in the week.
Is early morning or late afternoon a better time to see you
for about twenty minutes?

ROTH. I tell you I haven't any time to give to salesmen! ! !

ME *(fully a minute passes, while I am interested in ex-
amining one of his products set up on the floor).* Do you
make these, Mr. Roth?

ROTH. Yes.

ME *(another minute looking it over).* How long have you
been in this business, Mr. Roth?

ROTH. Oh . . . twenty-two years.

ME. How did you ever happen to get started in this
business?

ROTH *(leans back from work at desk, begins to warm up).*
Well, that's a long story. I went to work for John Doe Company when I was seventeen, worked my head off for them
for ten years, wasn't getting anywhere, so I struck out for
myself.

ME. Were you born here in Cheltenham, Mr. Roth?

ROTH *(getting warmer).* No. I was born in Switzerland.

ME *(pleasantly surprised).* Is that so? You must have
come over here when you were very young.

ROTH *(very friendly . . . smiling).* Well, I left home when
I was fourteen. Lived in Germany for a while. Then I decided I wanted to come to America.

ME. It must have taken a lot of capital to get a big plant like this started.

ROTH *(smiling)*. Well, I started this on $300, but worked it up to over $300,000!

ME. It must be very interesting to see the way these tanks are made.

ROTH *(gets up, goes over to tank where I am standing)*. Yes, we're pretty proud of our tanks. We believe they're the best on the market. Would you like to go through the plant and see how they're made?

ME. I'd love it!

(Roth puts hand on my shoulder and takes me out into the plant.)

This man's name is Ernest Roth, principal owner of Ernest Roth & Sons, Cheltenham, Pennsylvania. I didn't sell him on that first call. But over a period of sixteen years, I have made nineteen sales to him and six of his seven sons, that paid me well, and enabled me to form a mighty happy association with him.

POCKET REMINDERS

1. "If you would win a man to your cause, first convince him that you are his sincere friend. . . ." —Lincoln.

2. Encourage young men. Help a man see how he can be a success in life.

3. Try to get a man to tell you what is his greatest ambition in life. Help him raise his sights.

4. If anyone has inspired you, or helped you in any way, don't keep it a secret. Tell him about it.

5. Ask a man: "How did you happen to get started in this business?" then, *be a good listener.*

21. I BECAME MORE WEL-COME EVERYWHERE WHEN I DID THIS

→»» «←

AS A YOUNG man I had a major handicap that would have meant sure failure if I hadn't found a way to correct it quickly. I had the sourest puss you ever gazed on in all your life, and still have an old tintype to prove it. There was a reason.

My father died when I was a boy, leaving my mother with five small children, and no insurance. Mother had to take in washing and sewing to feed and clothe us and try to keep us in school. That was back in the "Gay Nineties," though they weren't very gay for us. Our little home was always cold; we never had heat anywhere but in the kitchen and we didn't even have a carpet on the floor. Children's epidemics ran wild in those days—smallpox, scarlet fever, typhoid fever, diphtheria—it seemed as though there was always one or more of us down with something. Haunted constantly by sickness, hunger, poverty, and death, my mother lost three of the five children during these epidemics. So you see we rarely had very much to smile about. In fact we were actually afraid to smile and act happy.

Soon after I started out to sell, I discovered that a worried,

147

sour expression brought results that were just about infallible—an unwelcome audience and failure.

It didn't take me long to realize that I had a serious handicap to overcome. I knew it wasn't going to be easy to change that worried expression on my face left by so many years of hardship. It meant a complete change in my outlook on life. Here is the method I tried. It began to show results *immediately* in my home, socially, and in business.

Each morning during a fifteen-minute bath and vigorous rubdown, I determined to cultivate a big, happy smile, just for that fifteen minutes. I soon discovered, however, that it couldn't be an insincere, commercialized smile, developed just for the purpose of putting dollars in my pocket. It had to be an honest-to-goodness smile from down deep inside, an outward expression of happiness from within!

No, it wasn't easy at first. Time and again I found myself during that fifteen-minute workout thinking thoughts of doubt, fear, and worry. Result? The old worried face again! A smile and worry simply won't mix, so once again I'd force the smile. Back came cheerful, optimistic thoughts.

Although I didn't realize it until later, this experience seems to substantiate the theory of the great philosopher and teacher, Professor William James of Harvard: "Action *seems* to follow feeling, but really action and feeling go together; and by regulating the action, which is under the more direct control of the will, we can indirectly regulate the feeling, which is not."

Let's see how starting off with a good fifteen-minute workout of the smile muscles helped me during the day. Before entering a man's office I would pause for an instant and think of the many things I had to be thankful for, work up a great big, honest-to-goodness smile, and then enter the room with the smile just vanishing from my face. It was easy then to turn on a big, happy, smile. Seldom did it fail to get the same kind of smile in return from the person I met on the inside. When Miss Secretary went in to the boss and announced me I feel sure she reflected some part of the smiles we'd exchanged in the outer office, for she would usually come back still wearing that smile.

Let's assume for a moment that I had gone in looking worried, or forcing one of those rubber-band smiles—you know, the kind that snaps right back—don't you think that secretary's expression would have practically told her boss *not* to see me? Then walking into the boss's office, it was natural for me to give him a happy smile as I said: "Mr. Livingston! Good morning!"

I've found it pleases people when I pass them on the street to give them a big, cheerful smile, and merely say: "Mr. Thomas!" It means so much more to them than the usual, "Good morning . . . how are you? . . . hello." If you know him well enough, try calling out just his first name "Bill!" with a grand, big smile.

Have you ever noticed that the breaks seem to go with the fellow who has a sincere, enthusiastic smile, and so frequently against the fellow who goes around looking dissatisfied, disgruntled and glum?

Telephone companies have proved by actual test the voice with a smile wins. Pick up your phone this instant, open your conversation with a big smile, and *feel the difference*. It might be a good idea if someone would invent a mirror that would be attached to the phone, so that we could *see* the difference.

I have asked thousands of men and women in audiences all over the country for a pledge to smile, *just for thirty days*, their happiest smile at every living creature they see. Easily 75 per cent of the people in each audience willingly raised their hands. What has been the result? I quote from one letter received from a Knoxville, Tennessee, man. It is typical of several letters which have come to me:

> My wife and I had just about agreed to separate. Of course, I thought she was entirely at fault. Within a few days after I began to put this idea into action, happiness was restored in my home. I then came to realize that I had been losing out in business because of a sullen, losing attitude. At the end of the day, I would go home and take it out on my wife and children. It was all my fault, not my wife's at all. I am a totally different man from what I was a year ago. I'm happier because I've made others happy too. Now everybody greets me with a smile. In addition my business has shown surprising improvement.

This man was so excited about the results he got from smiling, that he kept writing me for years about it!

Dorothy Dix has said: "There is no other weapon in the whole feminine armory to which men are so vulnerable as they are to a smile. . . . It is a thousand pities that women put no stress on cheerfulness as either a virtue or a duty, because there is no other quality that goes so far toward making marriage a success and keeping a husband nailed to his fireside. There is no man who doesn't hasten his footsteps to his own home at night if he knows he is going to find in it a woman whose smile makes sunshine within it."

I know it may sound incredible that you can cultivate happiness with a smile, but try it just for thirty days. Give every living soul you meet the *best* smile you ever smiled in your life, even your own wife and children, and see how much better you feel and look. It's one of the best ways I know to stop worrying, and start living. When I began doing this, I found I became more welcome everywhere.

22. HOW I LEARNED TO REMEMBER NAMES AND FACES

❧❧❧   ❦❦❦

ONE YEAR I taught a sales course at the Central Y.M.C.A., 1421 Arch Street, Philadelphia. During the course, we had a memory expert come in and give us three nights of memory training. That training made me realize how important it is to remember a man's name.

Since then I have read books and heard several lectures on the subject. In business and social contacts, I have tried to apply some of the ideas I learned. I found that I had much less difficulty remembering names and faces when I remembered these three things which all the experts teach:

1. *Impression.*
2. *Repetition.*
3. *Association.*

If you have any difficulty remembering these three rules, as I did, here's a simple little idea that made it impossible for me to forget them. I just thought of the name *Ira*. I-R-A are the first letters of these three words. Let's take a little time to analyze each one:

1. Impression

Psychologists tell us that most of our memory troubles are really not memory troubles at all; they are *observation* troubles. I guess that was largely my trouble. I seemed to observe a man's face pretty well, but usually failed completely in getting his name. Either I didn't listen when being introduced or I was unable to hear the name clearly. Guess what I did then? You're right. Nothing! I just skipped it as though the name meant nothing to me. But if the other person failed to pay any attention to *my* name, I felt hurt. If he took a real interest in my name, made sure he got it accurately, it never failed to please me. I became so much impressed with the importance of this first rule that I began thinking of it as an unpardonable discourtesy if I failed to listen attentively and get a name correctly.

How can you get it correctly? If you don't hear the name clearly it is perfectly proper to say: "Would you mind repeating your name?" Then if you are still not sure, it is proper to say: "I'm sorry, would you mind spelling it?" Is the other person ever offended by your genuine interest to know his name? I've never heard of it.

So the first thing that helped me to remember names and faces was to forget myself, and concentrate as hard as I could on the *other person*, his face, and his name. This helped me overcome self-consciousness when meeting strangers.

They say the eye actually takes a mental photograph of things we see and observe. It is easy to prove this because you can close your eyes and recall a stranger's face as clearly as though you were looking at a picture of him. You can do the same thing with a *name*.

I was surprised how much less difficulty I had in remembering names and faces, when I made a real effort to observe a man's face and get a *clear, vivid impression of his name*.

2. REPETITION

Do you ever forget a stranger's name within ten seconds after being introduced to him? I do unless I repeat it several times quickly while it is fresh in my mind. We can repeat his name immediately: "How do you do, Mr. Musgrave."

Then during the conversation, it helps me a lot if I use his name in some way: "Were you born in Des Moines, Mr. Musgrave?" If it is a difficult name to pronounce, it's better not to avoid it. Most people do that. If I don't know how to pronounce a name, I simply ask: "Am I pronouncing your name correctly?" I find people are glad to help you get their name right. If other people are present they are glad too; it makes it easier for them to understand the name and remember it.

Now, after doing that, you are on the spot if you forget a person's name, and I'm quite likely to forget it, unless I repeat the name silently to myself several times during the conversation, in addition to speaking it aloud.

Likewise, if you want to make sure that he remembers your name, you can usually find an opportunity to repeat your own name—perhaps something like this: ". . . and he said to me, 'Mr. Bettger, we've just had one of the best years.'"

Frequently, after I've left a man, I write his name down at the first opportunity. Just seeing the name written out is a big advantage.

Being introduced to several people at the same time is a tough spot for anybody. Here's an idea I got from my friend, Henry E. Strathmann, prominent builders' supply and coal merchant of Philadelphia, which has helped me.

Henry once had a poor memory, but cultivated such a remarkable ability to remember names, faces, and facts, that he makes a hobby of addressing large meetings, demonstrating his methods. Let me quote Mr. Strathmann:

> In meeting groups, try to get three or four names at a time, and take a few moments to assimilate them before trying the next group. Try to form a sentence of some of their names, to fasten them in your mind. Example: last week at a dinner, where I identified about fifty in a group of men and women, the guests at one table were introduced by the toastmaster. The following names were called: "Castle" . . . "Kammerer" . . . "Owens" . . . "Goodwin" . . . "Keyser." This was duck soup for making up a sentence, and when identifying the audience later, I showed them the power of association with the following: "It brings back a picture of World War I. The *Kaiser Owned* a *Castle*. The *Camera* showed it was a *Goodwin*. . . . These are very effective and stay with you a long time. They are not always so made to order, but if you are on the alert for them, it is surprising how often they occur. In groups of one or two, many puns are easily brought to mind, which hold the impression for you.

I used this idea to advantage just recently. I met with a committee of four dentists. The chairman, Dr. Howard K. Mathews, introduced me. He said: "Mr. Bettger, shake hands with Dr. Dolak, Dr. Green, and Dr. Hand." As I shook hands, I imagined the disciple, St. Matthew had returned to life as a prominent dentist, and was serving as chairman of this committee. Dr. *Mathews lacked the dough,* but *Dolak* had plenty of the *Green* stuff in his *Hand.*

Forming this silly story-sentence made it *easy* for me to use each doctor's name during the meeting. Just as Henry Strathmann told me, I find these pictures stay with me a long time.

Have you ever been embarrassed by being unable to introduce people, because someone's name escaped you momentarily? I don't know of any formula that will overcome such a failing. There are several things, however, which have helped me improve my ability to recall names more readily.

First—*Don't be overanxious.* It is a situation that can happen to anybody, and frequently does. I found the best thing is to laugh it off and admit frankly that I must be panicky. Groucho Marx laughed it off recently by saying: "I never forget a face, but in your case I'll make an exception!"

Second—*Whenever you pass someone you know call him by name.* Say "Mr. Follansbee! or Charles!" instead of merely "Hello" or "How are you?" Then after he is gone, repeat to yourself his full name a few times: "Charles L. Follansbee . . . Charles L. Follansbee."

Since people *do* like to hear their names spoken why not make it a habit to call everybody by name on every opportunity, whether it is the president of your company, a neighbor, bootblack, waiter, caddie, or Pullman porter. I never cease to be surprised at the difference it makes with people. And I found as I called more people by name, my memory for remembering names became better.

Third—*Whenever possible, take time beforehand to become familiar with a name.* Memory experts do this. Before speaking at a luncheon or dinner, they obtain a membership list of the organization and study the names and businesses. Then during the meeting the expert has one of the members point these people out in the audience. When he gets up to speak, he amazes everyone with his ability to identify members, designating each one by his full name and business.

In a smaller way we can use the same idea. Here's what I mean. Years ago when I was a member and regular attendant of the Ben Franklin Club and the Optimist Club, I was ashamed at my inability to speak to members, men I knew, by name. Then I began making it a habit to review the membership list before attending meetings. Soon I gained so much confidence in my new ability to recall names promptly that I found myself going around handshaking instead of avoiding members. I began making *friends* of these men instead of merely having a nodding acquaintance.

The real secret of repetition is: repetition at intervals. Make a list of people you want to remember, or *anything* you want to remember, and go over it briefly just before going to sleep, first thing in the morning, the next day, again next week. I believe you can remember almost anything, if you will only repeat it often enough, and at intervals.

3. ASSOCIATION

Now how can you retain what you want to remember? Association is undoubtedly the most important single factor.

We all amaze ourselves at times by our ability to recall things that occurred back in our early childhood, things we hadn't thought of since, and apparently had forgotten. For instance, recently I drove into a large service station in Ocean City, New Jersey, to get some gasoline. The owner of the station recognized me although it had been more than forty years since we'd met. I was embarrassed because I couldn't recall ever having laid eyes on the man before.

Now watch how the power of association began to operate.

"I'm Charles Lawson," the man said eagerly. "We went to James G. Blaine Grammar School together."

Well his name didn't sound familiar, and I would have been sure he was mistaken, if he hadn't called me by name, and mentioned James G. Blaine Grammar School. But my face still registered blank, so he continued: "Do you remember Bill Green? . . . do you remember Harry Schmidt?"

"Harry Schmidt! Certainly!" I answered. "Harry is one of my best friends."

"Don't you remember the morning Blaine School closed because of a smallpox epidemic and a crowd of us went out to Fairmount Park and chose up sides for a ball game?

You and I played on the same side. You played short, and I played second base."

"Chuck Lawson!" I yelled as I jumped out of my car and shook his hand violently. Chuck Lawson had applied the power of association, and it worked like magic!

HELPING OTHER PEOPLE TO REMEMBER YOUR NAME

Do people have difficulty remembering your name? Once I thought to myself: "Look here, Bettger, you've got a queer name yourself. Why not help the other fellow out a little?" With a little thought, I hit on this idea: when being introduced, or on introducing myself, I repeat my name, then with a grin, I say: "Pronounced like 'bet-cher life!' Bettger." Usually this gets a smile, and the stranger repeats: "You bet-cher life!" If it's a business introduction I say: "Like 'Bet-cher Life Insurance . . . Bettger." When I give my name over the phone, in a place I haven't been in touch with for months, the phone operator or secretary frequently says: "Oh, yes, Mr. 'Bet-cher' life!"

I believe most people really want to remember your name, and are embarrassed by not being able to recall it. If you can suggest an easy way for them to master and remember it, they are pleased.

When meeting anyone we haven't seen for a long time, I think it is best to mention our own name immediately. For example: "How are you, Mr. Jones, Tom Brown is my name. I used to see you frequently at the Penn A. C." This avoids any chance for embarrassment. I find people like that.

The other fellow will often help you to remember his name, if you frankly ask him how. Let me give one typical example: Recently I met many new people in Tulsa, Oklahoma. One man's name, S. R. Clinkscales, seemed to give me trouble. A review of our introduction will illustrate how he made it easy for me:

BETTGER. Would you mind repeating your name?

(The stranger repeated his name, but it sounded to me something like "Clykztuz.")

BETTGER. I'm sorry, would you mind spelling it?

STRANGER. C-l-i-n-k-s-c-a-l-e-s.

BETTGER. Clinkscales. That's an unusual name. I don't believe I ever heard it before. Is there some way I can remember it easily?

Was he offended? Not in the least. Grinning, he said: "Just imagine you see me being thrown in the *clink* holding a big set of *scales* in my hands . . . *Clink-Scales!*"

Silly? Sure! That's the reason it's good. He gave me an action picture. It would be impossible for me to forget him or his name, *Clink-Scales!*

Later I met "Clink" unexpectedly in Enid, Oklahoma, and greeted him instantly by name. "Clink" really was pleased, and of course, I was too.

If a name is extremely difficult to master, I ask about its history. Many foreign names have a romantic history behind them. Anyone would much rather discuss his name than the weather, and it's a thousand times more interesting.

Sometimes the reward for remembering names is out of all proportion to the extra effort you put into it. An old friend of mine who is too modest to let me use his name told me he learned the name of every manager of the 441 "X" chain stores. He called each manager by his first name. Furthermore he made it a point to find out the names of their wives and children. When a new baby arrived, or whenever there was sickness or trouble, Bill went around to see if he could help.

Bill had come over from Ireland to America when he was nineteen and took a job sweeping out one of the chain stores and keeping it clean. He became vice-president of the company some years later and retired a wealthy man when he was fifty-two.

Remembering names and faces wasn't the reason why Bill became vice-president, but he believes it was one of the important rungs in the ladder.

I asked him if he'd ever taken a memory course. "No," he laughed. "At first when my memory wasn't so good, I carried a large notebook. In ordinary, friendly conversation with a store manager, I found out the names of members of his family, even ages of his children. As soon as I got out in my car, I wrote down these names, and any other interesting facts. After a few years, I seldom found it necessary to refer to my notes, except for the newer employees."

In my work as a salesman, I've found it a great asset to remember not only the names of clients and prospects, but names of secretaries, phone operators and other associates.

Speaking to them by name makes them feel important. They *are* important! In fact, it's hard to overestimate the importance of their friendly co-operation.

I'm surprised at the large number of persons who tell me they cannot remember names, are constantly being distressed by it, but seem to feel there is nothing they can do about it. Why not make a little secret hobby out of it? In a comparatively short time you will find yourself enjoying a far better memory for names and faces than you ever hoped for. For one week carry a three-by-five card with you, with the following three rules written on it. Determine just for one week to apply these rules:

1. *Impression*   Get a clear impression of his name and face.
2. *Repetition*   Repeat his name at short intervals.
3. *Association*   Associate it with an action picture; if possible, include the person's business.

23. THE BIGGEST REASON WHY SALESMEN ◆ LOSE BUSINESS

〰〰 〰〰

BACK IN the days when Mark Twain was piloting boats up and down the Mississippi, the Rock Island Railroad decided to build a bridge across that great span between Rock Island, Illinois, and Davenport, Iowa. The steamboat companies were enjoying a great and prosperous commerce. Wheat, cured meats, and a few surplus products which our early settlers were able to produce were trekked to the Mississippi by ox teams and high-wheeled wagons, then shipped down the river. The steamboat owners looked upon their rights of transportation on the river as jealously as if they were God-given.

Fearing serious competition if the railroad succeeded in building the bridge, they entered an injunction in the courts to prevent its construction. Result: a big lawsuit. The wealthy steamboat owners hired Judge Wead, the best known river lawyer in the states. This case became one of the most important in the history of transportation.

On the closing day of the trial, the courthouse was jammed to capacity. Judge Wead, making his final talk to the court, held the crowd spellbound for two hours. He even hinted of a dissolution of the Union by reason of this fierce controversy. At the close of his oration, loud applause could be heard across the courthouse grounds.

When the lawyer for the Rock Island Railroad rose to speak, the audience felt sorry for him. Did he talk two hours? No! One minute. Here is substantially what he said: "First, I want to congratulate my opponent upon his wonderful oration. I have never heard a finer speech. But, gentlemen of the jury, Judge Wead has obscured the main issue. After all, the demands of those who travel from east to west are no less important than those who navigate up and down the river. The only question for you to decide is whether man has more right to travel up and down the river, than he has to cross the river."

Then he sat down.

It didn't take the jury long to reach a decision, a decision in favor of this poorly dressed, long, lanky obscure country lawyer. His name was Abraham Lincoln.

I am a great admirer of Abraham Lincoln, and one reason I am is because he came to the point so quickly. He was a master of brevity. He made the most famous address in the history of the world. The man who preceded him to the platform spoke for two hours. Then Lincoln spoke—for exactly *two minutes*. Nobody remembers what Edward Everett said, but Abraham Lincoln's Gettysburg Address will live forever. Everett's opinion of the speech Lincoln delivered was written in a note to Lincoln the next day. It was more than courtesy: *I should be glad if I could flatter myself that I came as near to the central idea of the occasion in two hours, as you did in two minutes.*

Years ago, I had the rare privilege of meeting and getting acquainted with James Howard Bridge, author and lecturer, who, as a young man, had been confidential secretary to Herbert Spencer, the great English philosopher. He told me that Herbert Spencer had a hair-trigger temper; that at the boarding house in London where Spencer lived, there frequently was a great deal of inconsequential chatter at the table. Spencer determined to outsmart his friends who talked too long. He invented ear pads similar to those now commonly used in zero weather. When the talk became too boring, he ended it for himself by taking out the pads from his coat-tail pocket, and slipping them on!

Overtalking is one of the worst of all social faults. If you have it, your best friend won't tell you, but he'll dodge you. I am writing on this subject because this very fault has been one of the biggest fights in my life. Lord knows, if there ever was a man who talked too much, it was this guy, Frank Bettger.

One of my best friends took me aside one time and said: "Frank, I can't ask you a question without your taking fifteen minutes to answer it, when it should only take one sentence!" But the thing that really shook me awake was the time I was interviewing a busy executive, and he said: "Come to the point! Never mind all those details." He didn't care anything about the arithmetic. He wanted the answer.

I got to thinking about the sales I had probably lost, the friends I had bored and the time I had lost. I was so impressed with the importance of learning to be brief that I asked my wife to hold up her finger whenever I got off the beam. I tried to avoid details as I would avoid a rattlesnake. Finally, as the months went by, I learned to talk less, but it is still a battle. In fact, I expect to keep on fighting that battle as long as I live. Just the other day I found myself talking for a quarter of an hour after I had said everything, simply because I was so full of the desire of talking.

How are your terminal facilities? Do you ever get "wound up" and can't stop? Do you ever catch yourself going into too much detail? Whenever you become conscious of talking too long—stop! "Set off the alarm clock" on yourself. If your listener doesn't insist on your finishing, then you know you've been dragging it out.

A salesman cannot *know* too much but he can *talk* too much. General Electric's vice-president Harry Erlicher, one of the biggest buyers in the world, says: "At a recent meeting of purchasing agents, we took a vote to find out the biggest reason why salesmen *lose* business. It is very significant the vote was three to one that *salesmen talk too much.*"

I can tell you how I cut my telephone conversations in half. Before I call a man, I make a list of things I want to talk about. Then I call him up and say: "I know you are busy. There are just four things I want to take up with you, and I'll do it one at a time . . . one........ two........ three........ four........"

When I finish number four, he knows the conversation is about over and that I am ready to hang up after he's answered me. And I end my conversation right there with: "All right, thanks so much." And hang up.

I don't mean we should be abrupt. We quickly resent the person who is abrupt; but we admire the person who is brief and to the point.

That great writer of Genesis told the story of the creation of the world in 442 words, less than half the number I have used in this chapter. There is a masterpiece of brevity!

24. THIS INTERVIEW TAUGHT ME HOW TO OVERCOME MY FEAR OF APPROACHING BIG MEN

>» «<

SOMEONE asked me the other day if I had ever been scared? *Scared* is no word for it. I was terrified! It happened long ago when I was struggling along eking out a bare existence trying to sell life insurance. Gradually it dawned on me that if I wanted to become more successful, I'd have to call on some bigger people and sell larger policies. In other words, I'd been playing in the bush leagues, and now I wanted to try the majors.

The first big-shot call I made was on Archie E. Hughes, president of the Foss-Hughes Company, of Philadelphia, located at 21st and Market Streets. He was one of the leaders in the automobile industry on the Eastern seaboard. Mr. Hughes was a busy man. I had tried several times to get in to see him.

As his secretary ushered me into his luxuriously furnished office I became increasingly nervous. My voice trembled as I began to speak. Suddenly I lost my nerve completely and just couldn't go on. There I stood, shaking with fear. Mr. Hughes looked up in astonishment. Then, without knowing it, I did a wise thing, a simple little thing that

168

turned the interview from a ridiculous failure to success. I stammered, "Mr. Hughes . . . I . . . uh . . . I've been trying to see you for a long while . . . and, uh . . . now that I'm here, I'm so nervous and scared I can't talk!"

Even while I spoke, to my surprise, my fear began to leave me. My dazed head quickly cleared, my hands and knees stopped shaking. Mr. Hughes suddenly seemed to become my friend. He obviously was pleased, pleased that I should regard him as such an important individual. A kindly expression came over his face as he said, "That's perfectly all right. Take your time. I've felt the same way myself many times when I was a young man. Sit down and take it easy."

He tactfully encouraged me to go on by asking me questions. *It was apparent if I had an idea which he could use, he was definitely going to help me make the sale.*

I didn't sell Mr. Hughes, but I gained something which later proved to be far more valuable than the commission I would have made on that sale. I discovered this simple rule. Here it is: *When you're scared . . . admit it!*

This fear complex of being afraid to talk to important people I thought was due to a lack of courage. I was ashamed of it. I tried to keep it a secret. I have learned since, however, that many successful men, prominent in public affairs, are haunted by the same fears. For example, early in the spring of 1937, at the Empire Theater, New York City, I was astonished to hear Maurice Evans (regarded by many critics as the world's greatest Shakespearean actor) confess nervousness to a large audience of parents and graduating students of the American Academy of Dramatic Art. I happened to be there because my son Lyle was in that class.

Mr. Evans was the principal speaker of the occasion. After saying a few words, he faltered, obviously embarrassed, then said: "I'm terrified. I didn't realize I was going to speak to such a large and important-looking audience. I planned what I thought would be some appropriate things to say, but they have all left me."

The audience loved Maurice Evans for it. Admitting openly that he was terrified, seemed to break the strain. He regained his composure, went on and thrilled young and old by talking to them right out of his heart.

During the war, I heard a U. S. naval officer speak at a war bond rally luncheon at the Bellevue-Stratford Hotel in Philadelphia. Here was a man who had distinguished himself by his courage and bravery in the Solomons. The audience anticipated a speech filled with excitement and blood-curdling experiences. As he rose, he took some papers from his pocket, and, much to the dismay of the crowd began to read his speech. He was extremely nervous, but was trying to hide it from his audience. His hand trembled so badly that he read with difficulty. Suddenly, his voice faded out. Then with embarrassment but sincere humility, he said: "I'm much more frightened right now, facing this audience, than I ever was facing the Japs at Guadalcanal."

After this honest confession, he ignored his notes completely and began speaking with confidence and enthusiasm. He was a hundred times more interesting and effective.

This naval officer found just what Maurice Evans had found, what I have found, and what thousands of others have found—when you're in a tight spot and scared to death, admit it! When you're in a bad spot and you're wrong, just admit it 100 per cent.

I wrote an article on this subject in 1944 for *Your Life* magazine. Shortly after it was published I was thrilled to receive the following letter:

> Somewhere in the Pacific
> September 11, 1944
>
> Dear Frank Bettger:
>
> I have just finished reading and thinking over an article by you in the September issue of *Your Life* magazine. You entitled your article, "When You Are Scared, Admit It!" and I have been thinking over just how good that advice is—especially out here with a soldier in a combat area.
>
> I have naturally had experiences similar to those you relate. Public speeches in high school and in college; conferences with employers before and after obtaining a job; the first serious talk with that certain young woman—all these have caused me to be scared, and greatly so.
>
> Well perhaps you wonder why I write to you from out here to second your statements because certainly I'm not giving public speeches or asking for a job. No, I'm not subjected to ordeals from that direction, but believe me I do know what fear is and how it affects a person. And also, we have found that your advice, "Admit it!" is absolutely just as appropriate and right when you are facing a Jap demon assault.

It has been proven time and time again out here that the men who fail to admit their fear are the ones who crack in battle. But if you admit you are scared, damned scared, and don't try to fight it down, then you are on the right road to overcoming your fear in most cases.

And now, thank you for writing that article, and I sincerely hope that those lucky students and workers who have the opportunity to make use of your advice will certainly do so.

Sincerely,
Charles Thompson

16143837 Co. C
382 Infantry U. S. Army
A.P.O. #96, c/o Postmaster, San Francisco, Calif.

This letter from out there on the firing line was certainly written under the most dire circumstances, yet, there are probably people right now, reading this chapter, who have walked up and down time and time again in front of a man's office door, trying to get up enough courage to go in. Are you one of them? Big men—their wives don't tremble in their presence! You pay a big compliment to a man when you tell him you are scared in his presence.

As I look back at it now, I realize what a fool I was, how many times I failed to take advantage of opportunities, because I was afraid to talk to important people. Calling on Archie Hughes was an important step in my selling career. I dreaded to go in to see him, and was terrified when I got in. If I hadn't admitted I was scared I would have gone out of there whipped! That one experience helped me to get into a higher income bracket. It showed me that this man really was a simple, approachable man, after all, even though he was big. In fact, this was one of the reasons he was so big.

There is no disgrace in admitting you are scared, but there is disgrace in failing to *try*. So whether you're talking to one person, or a thousand, if that strange demon fear, public enemy number one, suddenly steals up on you, and you find yourself too scared for words, remember this simple rule:

WHEN YOU'RE SCARED, ADMIT IT.

SUMMARY

PART FOUR

POCKET REMINDERS

1. "If you would win a man to your cause," said Abraham Lincoln, "first convince him that you are his sincere friend."

2. If you want to be welcome everywhere, give every living soul you meet a smile, an honest-to-goodness smile, from down deep inside.

3. You will have much less difficulty remembering names and faces when you remember these three things:
   a. *Impression:* Get a clear impression of his name and face.
   b. *Repetition:* Repeat his name at short intervals.
   c. *Association:* Associate his name with an action picture if possible; include his business.

4. Be brief. A salesman cannot *know* too much, but he can *talk* too much. General Electric's vice-president, Harry Erlicher, said: "At a recent meeting of purchasing agents, we took a vote to find out the biggest reason why salesmen lose business. It is very significant the vote was three to one that salesmen *talk too much*."

5. If you have any fear of approaching big men, turn that liability into an asset! Go to see the man you're afraid to call on, and *admit* you're scared. You pay a big compliment to a man when you tell him you are scared in his presence. If you have an idea he can use, he will *help* you make the sale.

Part Five

STEPS IN THE SALE

⫸ ⫷

25. ♦ THE SALE BEFORE THE SALE

⊨»» «««

ONE TIME while standing on the deck of a large ship, watching it dock at Miami, Florida, I saw something which taught me an important lesson I needed to learn badly about approaching the prospect. Right at that time selling was the farthest thing from my mind. I was on vacation.

As the ship moved closer to the pier, one of the crew heaved something that looked like a baseball with a thin rope attached to it. An attendant standing on the pier stretched his arms wide apart, but let the ball pass over his head, allowing the rope to fall down over one arm. As he pulled the line hand over hand onto the deck, I noticed it was dragging a much thicker rope through the water and onto the pier. Soon the attendant was able to curl the heavy rope around an upright iron post, the bollard. Gradually the ship was drawn up alongside of the pier and made fast to the dock.

I asked the captain about this. He said: "That small rope is called the 'heaving line,' the ball attached to it is called the 'monkey's fist,' the heavy rope which fastens the ship to

179

the dock is the 'hawser.' It would be impossible to throw the hawser far enough over the side of the ship to make connection with the pier."

Right there it dawned on me why I had been losing too many promising looking prospects on my approach. I had been trying to throw them the hawser. For example, just a few days before, a wholesale baker had threatened to throw me off the delivery platform of his bakery. I had barged in without an appointment, and began delivering a sales talk before he understood who I was, whom I represented, or what I wanted. No wonder he was so discourteous. He simply returned what I had given him. Now, I wondered how I could ever have been so stupid!

After I returned home from that vacation, I began reading everything I could find on "The Approach." I asked older and more experienced salesmen about it. I was surprised to hear some of them say: "The approach is the most difficult step in the sale!"

I began to understand why I got so nervous and frequently paced up and down in front of an office door before going in to see a man. I didn't know *how* to approach him! I was afraid of being turned down without having an opportunity to tell my story.

Now where do you suppose I got some of the best advice on how to approach? Not from salesmen at all. I got it by asking the *prospects* themselves. Here are two things I learned from them that helped me:

1. They dislike salesmen who keep them in suspense about who they are, whom they represent,

and what they want. They resent it violently if a salesman uses subterfuge, attempts to camouflage, or gives a false impression of the nature of his business or the purpose of his call. They admire the salesman who is natural, sincere, and honest in his approach, and who comes right to the point about the purpose of his call.

2. If the salesman calls without an appointment, they like him to ask if it is convenient to talk now, rather than start right off on a sales talk.

Years later, I heard my friend, Richard (Dick) Borden, of New York City, one of the nation's outstanding sales lecturers and counsellors, tell salesmen: "There is little use telling a sales story to a prospect who hasn't first been sold on the importance of listening to you. So use the first ten seconds on every call to purchase the time you need to tell your complete story. Sell the *interview*, before you attempt to sell the product."

If I should drop in on a man, without an appointment, I simply say: Mr. Wilson, my name is Bettger, Frank Bettger, of the Fidelity Mutual Life Insurance Company. Your friend, Vic Ridenour, asked me to stop in and see you the next time I was in your neighborhood. Can you talk for a few minutes now, or would you rather I call later?"

Usually he will say: "Go ahead" or, "What did you want to talk to me about?"

"You!" is my reply.

"What about me?" he generally asks.

Right there is the critical moment of the approach. If you're not prepared to answer this question immediately, and satisfactorily, you had better not make the call at all!

If you indicate that you want to sell him something that will cost him money, you are virtually telling him that you want to increase his problems. He is already worrying about how to pay all the bills in his desk-drawer, and how to hold down his expenses. If you want to discuss some vital problem of his, he is anxious to talk with an open mind about any idea that may help him solve that problem. The housewife doesn't have time to talk to a salesman about buying a new refrigerator, but she is worried about the high cost of meat, butter, eggs, milk. She is vitally interested in hearing about how she can cut down waste, and reduce the cost of food. A busy young man is not interested in joining the Junior Chamber of Commerce, but he is tremendously interested in making more friends, becoming better known, more highly regarded in his community, and in the possibility of increasing his income.

Sometimes a successful approach is made without any "approach talk" at all. Let me give just a few examples: Recently at my home one evening, a personal friend, long associated with an outstanding manufacturing concern, told me this story:

"It was my first trip as a salesman out of Philadelphia. I had never been to New York City. The last stop before getting to the big town was Newark. When I entered my prospect's store he was busy with a customer. His little five-year-old daughter was playing on the floor. She was a sweet little thing and we became friends in no time at all. I played pick-a-back with her around and around the bundles of merchandise. When the baby's daddy was free, and I introduced myself, he remarked: 'We haven't bought anything from your company for a long time.' I didn't talk business to him. I only talked about his little daughter. He said: 'I see you like my little girl. Would you like to come back tonight and join the birthday party we are giving her? We live just above the store here.'

"On I went to get my first glimpse of New York, and it was only that—just a glimpse. After checking into the old Seville, and washing up a bit, I returned to Newark and the party. Every minute of the evening was delightful. I stayed until midnight. When I began to leave I had a great thrill when I was handed the biggest order that customer ever gave our house. I didn't try to sell anything. Just by taking time out to be nice to a nice little girl I was building up the sort of approach which never fails to pay off."

That salesman is too modest to let me use his name, but he went on to become sales manager, then general manager, and finally president of his company, a company which has proved its mettle for well over one hundred years. "In my twenty-five years of selling," he went on to tell me, "the best approach I ever found was to first find out about a prospect's hobby, and then talk about that hobby."

You don't always have a baby to play with, or a hobby to talk about, but there is always a way to be friendly. I was having lunch recently with another personal friend of mine, Lester H. Shingle, president of the Shingle Leather Company, Camden, New Jersey. Lester is one of the ablest salesmen I have ever known. He said:

"Many years ago, when I was a young salesman, I called on a large manufacturer in New York state, but never was successful in selling him. One day, as I entered this older man's office, he acted annoyed and said: 'I'm sorry, but I can't give you any time today. I'm just going out to lunch.'

"Realizing that some unusual approach was necessary, and quick, I said: 'Would you mind taking me to lunch, Mr. Pitts?' He seemed somewhat surprised, but said, 'Sure, come along.'

"I didn't say a word to him about business, while we ate lunch. After we got back to his office he gave me a small order. It was the first we had ever received from him, but it proved to be the beginning of a good line of business that continued for many years."

In May of 1945, I was in Enid, Oklahoma. While there, I heard of a retail shoe salesman named Dean Niemeyer who had just established what may have been a world's record by selling 105 pairs of shoes in one day. Each sale was a separate, individual sale, made to 87 women and children. Here was a man I wanted to talk to, so I went around to the store where Mr. Niemeyer worked and asked him how he did it. He said: "It is all in the approach. A customer is either sold or missed by the way she is approached at the front door."

I was anxious to see just what he meant, so I watched him in action part of that morning. He really makes the customer feel at home. He goes out and meets her at the door with a sincere, warm-hearted smile. With Dean's natural, easy, helpful manner, the customer feels glad she came into the store. *She is sold before she sits down.*

These three men simply applied in their approach the first, and probably the most important, step in selling anything: "Sell yourself first!"

I've found that what I do in the approach usually determines where I stand in the mind of the prospect: "order taker" or "adviser." If my approach is right, then when I give my sales presentation I am master of the interview. If I fail in my approach, the prospect is master of the interview.

I am going to close this chapter with the approach talk I use—a talk developed over a period of years, which became invaluable to me. I must depend on you to translate some part of it into your own particular field of selling.

Me. Mr. Kothe, I can't tell by the color of your hair or the color of your eyes what your situation is, any more than a doctor could diagnose my condition if I walked into his office, sat down and refused to talk. That doctor couldn't do much for me, could he?

Mr. Kothe (*usually with a grin*). No, that's right.

Me. Well, that's my position with you, unless you are willing to take me into your confidence to a certain degree. In other words, in order that I may show you something at a future date that might be of value to you, would you mind if I ask you a few questions?

Mr. Kothe. Go ahead. What are the questions?

Me. Now if I ask you some questions you do not care to answer, you won't offend me. I'll understand. But if anybody knows anything about what you tell me, it will be because *you* tell them, not because *I* do. It is in strict confidence.

THE QUESTIONNAIRE

I find that I get into the questions more smoothly by waiting until my prospect is answering my first question before removing the questionnaire from my pocket. I do this while I am looking straight at him and listening with great interest. I developed the questionnaire over a long period of years. It is brief but it gives me a complete picture of the prospect's situation; also some idea of his immediate plans and future objectives. I go through the questions as rapidly as possible. It takes me from five to ten minutes, depending on how much he talks.

Here are some of the intimate questions that I do not hesitate to ask:

> What minimum monthly income would your wife need
>   in the event of your death?
> Minimum monthly income for yourself at age sixty-five?
> What is the present value of your estate?
> Stocks, bonds, other securities?
> Real estate? (mortgages)
> Cash on hand?
> Earned annual income?
> Your life insurance?
> How much do you pay out each year for insurance?

You need have no fear of asking the same kind of intimate questions that apply directly to your particular business if you prepare your prospect for them with an approach talk similar to the one I have given above.

I put the paper back in my pocket in the same manner that I take it out. My last question is (with a smile) "What do you do when you are not working, Mr. Kothe? In other words, do you have a hobby?"

His answer to this question frequently becomes valuable to me at a later date. While he is answering that question I return the questionnaire to my pocket. I never show it to the prospect in the first interview. His curiosity in the meantime will develop to such an extent that it will improve my chances in the second interview. After I complete the information, I get out as soon as I can. I say: "Thank you for your confidence, Mr. Kothe. I am going to give this some thought. I think I've got an idea that may be of value to you, and after I work it out, I'll give you a call for an appointment. Is that satisfactory?" And his answer generally is: "Yes."

I use my judgment as to whether I should arrange a definite appointment at that very moment, for a later date, say for the following week.

IMPORTANT. These questionnaires should be kept in a file, just like a doctor keeps a complete record of his patients. It provides you with information about your customer that progresses with the success of the man himself. And I have found as these men grow they look forward to telling you about their progress. They know, when you are sincerely interested, that you are one person with whom they can discuss their problems, and share their success and happiness.

I don't believe the approach talk should be memorized. But I *do* believe it should be written out and read several times each day. Then suddenly, one day, you know it. If you learn it that way it will never sound canned. Give your talk to your wife. Rehearse it over and over with her, until you know it so well it becomes part of you.

SUMMED UP

1. Don't try to throw the "hawser"—throw the "heaving line."

2. The approach must have only one objective: selling the sales interview, not your product, your *interview*. It is the *sale before the sale*.

26. THE SECRET OF MAKING APPOINTMENTS

➳➳➳ ⫷⫷⫷

I HAVE been going to the same barber every week for the past thirty-one years, a little Italian, named Ruby Day. An uncle started him out as an apprentice when he was only nine years old. He was so short he had to stand on a stool. Ruby's customers think he is probably one of the world's best barbers. In addition he is a ray of sunshine.

In spite of these qualities, back in 1927, Ruby was going down hill fast. His business had become so bad, and he was so low financially, he couldn't pay his rent for four months, and the owner of the building where he had his little one-man shop was threatening to throw him out.

One Friday afternoon, while he was cutting my hair, I noticed that he looked ill. I asked him what was wrong. And finally he confessed to me the awful fix he was in. On top of all this his wife had just given birth to a new baby boy, Ruby, Jr.

While we were talking, another customer stopped in and wanted to know how soon he could get fixed up. Ruby assured him it wouldn't be long, so reluctantly, the customer sat down and began reading one of the magazines.

I said: "Ruby, why don't you work by appointment?"

"Oh, Mr. Bettger," he replied, "I can't work by appointment; people won't make an appointment with a barber."

"Why not?" I asked.

"That's all right for a doctor, or lawyer," he said, "but people just won't make an appointment with a barber."

"I don't know why not," I insisted. "I thought the same thing about my business until another salesman convinced me it was the only way to work.

"Your customers like your work, Ruby, and they like you, but they don't like to wait. I'll bet this man here would be glad to make an appointment with you for a definite time each week, wouldn't you?"

"Sure!" nodded the customer.

He and Ruby quickly agreed on a standing date each week.

"There you are," I said enthusiastically. "Now put me down for eight every Friday morning."

The next day, Ruby had an appointment book, and began calling up all his old customers, many of whom hadn't been in his shop for months. Gradually he was able to get that appointment book dated up with a full schedule, and his financial worries became a thing of the past. For twenty years now he has worked exclusively by appointment. He trained his customers to expect it. They like it that way, because it saves them time. Today R. B. (Ruby) Day owns his beautiful little home *outright* at 919 Fox Chase Road, Hollywood, Penna. And he gives you the impression of being a substantial, happy business man.

I told this story one night in a sales school we were conducting in Pasadena, California. There was a taxi driver in the school. At the close of the week, he came backstage to see us and said: "I am a business man now!" We asked him what he meant. "Well," said he, "after I heard that talk on Tuesday night, I thought if a barber was able to make appointments, I should try it. The next morning, I took the president of a large company over to Glendale to catch a train. Driving over, I asked him how long he would be away. He said he'd be coming back the same night and agreed to let me take him home. That night he seemed pleased as I let him off at his home, and gave me a nice tip. I found out that he made this trip every week and sometimes found it hard to get a taxi. So I made a set date for this same job each week. Besides he gave me names of other executives of his company for me to call for appointments. When I phoned I told them I was calling at the suggestion of their president. By making these calls, I got two other jobs the following morning. Today, I bought an appointment book, and I'm going to build a list of *regular* jobs like your barber did. Now I feel like a business man!"

I made this same suggestion to my haberdasher. Soon most of his customers were coming in by definite appointment.

These men found just what I found and thousands of others in almost every line of business have found—people *prefer* to work by appointment!

1. It saves time, helps eliminate a lot of the tragic waste of time most salesmen worry about. Like-

wise it saves the customer's time.

2. By asking for an appointment, we let the customer know we realize he is busy. Instinctively
he places more value on our time. When I have
an appointment, I get a better hearing, and the
man has more respect for what I say.

3. It makes each call an event. An appointment
raises the salesman out of the class of a peddler.

My old roommate, Miller Huggins, was noted in baseball
for being a great lead-off man, because he got on base so
often. By getting on base so often, naturally, he scored
more runs on the average than most other players. In selling I found that making appointments is like getting on
base. The foundation of sales lies in getting interviews, and
the secret of getting good, attentive, courteous interviews, is
in selling appointments. Appointments are much easier to
sell than radios, vacuum cleaners, books, or insurance. After
I got that clear in my mind, a great relief came over me. I
stopped swinging for a home run. I merely tried to get on
first base!

When I phone someone I know, I simply ask for the appointment, and usually get it without being questioned. But
if it is someone I have never met, he invariably asks: "What
is it you want to see me about?"

There is the critical moment of the approach. As sure as I
indicate that I want to sell something, I'm licked right there,
and the chances of getting an appointment later are ruined.
The truth of it is, I may not know whether he needs what
I am selling. So the purpose of an appointment is merely
for a discussion. Yet even to this day I must be on my guard

not to allow myself to be drawn into a sales talk on the phone. I must concentrate on one thing, and one thing alone, selling an *appointment*.

Let me give you a typical example: The other day, I was able to get a man on the phone who has been traveling on business by plane at the rate of more than ten thousand miles every month. Here is our conversation:

ME. Mr. Aley, my name is Bettger, Frank Bettger, friend of Richard Flicker. You remember Dick, don't you?

ALEY. Yes.

ME. Mr. Aley, I am a life insurance salesman. Dick suggested that I ought to know you. I know you are busy, but I wonder if I may see you for about five minutes one day this week?

ALEY. What did you want to see me about—insurance? I just loaded up with more insurance a few weeks ago.

ME. That's all right, Mr. Aley. If I try to sell you anything, it will be your fault, not mine. May I see you for a few minutes tomorrow morning, say about nine o'clock?

ALEY. I have an appointment for nine-thirty.

ME. Well, if I take longer than five minutes, it will be your fault, not mine.

ALEY. All right. You'd better make it nine-fifteen.

ME. Thank you, Mr. Aley. I'll be there.

The next morning as I shook hands with him in his office, I took out my watch and said: "You've got another appointment at nine-thirty, so I'm going to limit myself to exactly five minutes."

I went through my questions as briefly as I could. When my five minutes were gone I said: "Well, my five minutes are up. Is there anything else you would like to tell me, Mr. Aley?" And for the next ten minutes Mr. Aley told me all that I really wanted to know about him.

I've had some men keep me as long as an hour over my five minutes telling me all about themselves; but it's never my fault, it's theirs! !

I know many successful salesmen who do not work by definite appointment when calling on their regular customers, but in questioning these salesmen, I find that they have regular days to call, and usually at about the same time of the day. In other words, they are *expected*.

"They won't come into the office." There used to be a sign on our office wall with those words in large print. I always believed it, too, until I heard Harry Wright, a dynamic salesman from Chicago, talk at a meeting one night. Harry discovered that they *will* come into the office. "I close sixty-five per cent of my business in my own office," he said. "I always suggest my office for the appointment, explaining that there will be no interruptions and we can conclude our business there more quickly and satisfactorily."

At first I was afraid of it. But I was surprised to find that many men preferred it that way. When they come into my office I never permit any interruptions. If my phone rings I answer something like this:

"Oh, hello, Vernon. Are you going to be there for a little while? May I call you back in about twenty minutes? I've got someone here and I don't want to hold him up. Thanks,

Vernon. I'll call you back." Then I click the phone and ask our girl outside to cut off all calls while Mr. Thomas is with me. This never fails to please my caller.

Before he leaves, if he is not in too big a hurry, I make it a point to introduce him around the office to people who have helped serve him, or who are likely to serve him if he becomes a client.

I know many salesmen who find this an excellent opportunity to take customers through their offices, plant or factory, and show them how their goods are produced.

DIFFICULT MEN TO SEE

Practice will improve anyone's technique in making appointments. Of course, there are always some men who are difficult to see. However, I've found them the *best* prospects if I can get to them. Just as long as I am courteous, I find they do not resent persistency. Here are a few questions I use, and ideas that have helped me:

1. "Mr. Brown, is there any best time to see you —early morning, or late afternoon?"
   "Is early in the week, or late in the week better?"
   "May I see you this evening?"

2. "What time do you go to lunch? Let's have lunch together one day this week. Will you have lunch with me tomorrow at the Union League, say about twelve or twelve-thirty?"

3. If he is extremely pressed for time, but sincere about being willing to see me, I sometimes ask: "Have you got your car in town today?"

If he says "no," I offer to drive him home in my car. I say: "It will give us a few minutes together."

4. I've been surprised how many men who are unwilling to make a definite appointment will agree to see me if I set the time far enough in advance. For example, on Friday mornings when I am planning my week's work ahead, if I phone and say: "Mr. Jones, I will be in your neighborhood next Wednesday, do you mind if I stop in and see you?" he will generally agree. Then I ask him whether morning or afternoon is better, and sometimes he will name an hour.

After making every reasonable effort, if I feel he is not sincere in trying to co-operate, I forget him.

Some of the best contacts I ever made were men who were extremely difficult to see. To illustrate: I was given the name of a contracting engineer in Philadelphia. After phoning a couple of times, I learned that he seldom was in his office except between 7 and 7:30 A.M.

The next morning I walked into his office at seven o'clock. It was in the dead of winter, and dark as night outside. He was glancing over some letters on his desk. Suddenly he grabbed a large brief-case and brushed right past me. I followed him out to his car. As he opened the trunk of his car, he looked at me and said: "What did you want to talk to me about?"

I said: "*You.*"

He said: "I can't stop this morning to talk with anybody."

"Where are you bound for this morning?" I asked.

"Collingswood, New Jersey," he replied.

"Let me chauffeur you down in my car," I suggested.

"No! I've got a lot of things in my car that I will need today," he replied.

"Would you mind if I sit alongside of you while you drive?" I asked. "We can talk while you drive. That will save your time."

"How will you get back?" he asked. "I'll be working my way down to Wilmington, Delaware."

"Let me worry about how I'll get back; that's no problem," I assured him.

"Come on. Get in," he grinned.

At that time he didn't even know my name or what I wanted to talk to him about, but I left him in Wilmington and returned to Philadelphia on a noon train with a signed order.

I have ridden on trains to Baltimore, Washington, and New York, with men I probably would never have been able to tie down to a definite appointment otherwise.

IMPORTANT THINGS I LEARNED ABOUT USING THE TELEPHONE

I got into the habit of always carrying plenty of nickels in my pockets so that I could use pay-station telephones wherever I might be. In fact many times I've walked out of my own office, and gone to a phone booth around the corner, simply because there were too many interruptions in my office.

After I set aside Friday morning for planning, I began

telephoning most of the people I wanted to call on the following week. It was astonishing sometimes how I could line up appointments for a large part of my week's itinerary.

It took me a long while to learn not to be afraid to leave word for a client, or even a prospect, to call me back. After calling him several times and failing to contact him, he got the impression that I was chasing him for something *I* wanted. I found that by leaving a message for him to call me, he got the impression that I must have something *he* wanted. Something important to *him*.

After I came to recognize the importance of first selling the appointment, I was able to get all the interviews I could handle.

Let me repeat once more the rule it took me so long to learn:

First, Sell the *appointment*

Second, Sell your product

27. HOW I LEARNED TO OUTSMART SECRETARIES AND SWITCHBOARD OPERATORS

→» «←

ONE DAY last week I listened to a superb lesson in how to outsmart secretaries and switchboard oper-ators. I was having lunch with our regular group at the Union League, when one of the members of our table, Donald E. Lindsay, president of the Murlin Manufacturing Company, Philadelphia, told us this story:

"A salesman came into our plant this morning and asked to see Mr. Lindsay. My secretary went out and asked him whether he had an appointment with Mr. Lindsay. 'No,' he said, 'I don't have an appointment, but I have some infor-mation for him that I know he will want.' My secretary asked him his name, and whom he represented. He told her his name, but said it was a personal matter. She said: 'Well I am Mr. Lindsay's private secretary. If it's something per-sonal, perhaps I can take care of it. Mr. Lindsay is very busy right now.'

" 'This is a *personal* matter,' insisted the man. 'I think I had better talk directly with Mr. Lindsay about it.'

"Right at that time," Don explained to us, "I happened to be in the back of the plant. My hands were grimy; I was working with two of our mechanics on something they'd been having trouble with. I washed my hands and came out to the front office."

"I didn't recognize the fellow, but he introduced himself, shook hands with me, and asked if he could see me in my private office for about five minutes. I asked him 'What about?' He said: 'It's entirely a personal matter, Mr. Lindsay, but I can tell you in a few minutes.'

"When we got back in my office, the man said: 'Mr. Lindsay, we have developed a tax-survey service that may save you considerable money. We make no charge for this service. All we need is some information from you which will be treated in the strictest confidence.'

"With that, he pulled out a questionnaire and started to ask me some questions. I said: 'Wait a minute. You've got something to sell me. Now what is it? Whom do you represent?'

" 'Pardon me, Mr. Lindsay,' he said, 'but . . .'

" 'What company do you represent?' I demanded.

" 'The A.B.C. Insurance Company. I . . .'

" '*Get out of here!*' I said. 'You've gotten in here by subterfuge. If you don't get out of here quick, I'll throw you out!' "

Don Lindsay had been on the wrestling team when he was a student at the University of Pennsylvania. Knowing Don, as most of us do, we had a big laugh, because Don really knows *how* to throw 'em out! As he told the story we could see by the way he colored up that it was a good thing the salesman left promptly.

This salesman made a very good appearance, and talked well, Don told us. But let's take just a few moments to analyze his approach:

1. He had no appointment. He caught Mr. Lindsay at an inopportune time, which usually is the case when you're not expected.
2. He told the secretary his name, which meant nothing, because he evaded her question: "Whom do you represent?" That always arouses suspicion.
3. When the secretary told him Mr. Lindsay was busy, he implied that he didn't believe her—which she resented.
4. He got in by *subterfuge*. He killed all chance of going back to that plant again. Although he represented a good company, he made it extremely difficult for *any* of their representatives to ever do business in that plant.

My experience in trying to get in to see busy prospects has taught me that it is more a matter of common sense than clever tricks. Many salesmen don't seem to realize that a man's secretary can be so important to them. In many cases, she is the power behind the throne. I learned that if I want to see the big shot, my best bet is to place myself in her hands, and usually, she'll guide me through to the sanctum sanctorum. After all she frequently is the big shot's boss so far as his time for appointments is concerned. When we work with a man's secretary, we are working with his "right hand." I find my punches go over better when I take her into my confidence, am honest and sincere with her, and show respect for her position.

In the beginning, I try to find out her name from someone else in the office. Then I always speak to her by name. I write her name down on a permanent record card so that I won't ever forget it. In phoning later, for an appointment, I usually say: "Miss Mallets, good morning! This is Mr. Bettger. I wonder if you could work me into Mr. Harshaw's schedule for twenty minutes today, or sometime this week?"

I realize that many secretaries and receptionists feel as though it is their duty to get rid of salesmen. But I don't believe trickery and subterfuge is the way to handle them. A clever man with a dominating personality may often get by the secretary without stating the purpose of his call. A salesman with lots of nerve and a fluent tongue may get away with it once in a while, but I believe the best way to outsmart secretaries and switchboard operators is never to try!

28. AN IDEA THAT HELPED ME GET INTO THE "MAJOR LEAGUES"

>>> <<<

I HAVE been surprised to find that many of the ideas I've used in selling I first learned in baseball. For instance, while I was playing with Greenville, South Carolina, the manager, Tommy Stouch, said to me one day: "Frank, if you could only hit, the big-league clubs would be after you."

"Is there any way I could learn to hit?" I asked.

"Jesse Burkett was no better hitter than you," declared Tom. "Yet he became one of the greatest hitters in baseball!"

"How did he ever do that?" I asked, doubtfully.

"Burkett made up his mind he was going to learn *how* to hit," said Tommy, "so he went out to the ball park every morning and hit three hundred balls. He paid some boys a few nickels to chase them while one boy pitched 'em up. Jesse didn't try to slug the ball, but he practiced a free, smooth swing, until his timing became perfect."

That story sounded too good. I had to see it for myself. So I looked up the records: only *two* players ever had batted over .400 in more than one season. One of them was Lajoie. The other was Jesse Burkett!

204

I got so excited about the idea I tried to get a few of the other players on the team to try it with me, but they told me I was crazy. They said a Northerner just couldn't stand the hot Southern sun both morning and afternoon. But my roommate, Ivy (Reds) Wingo, a catcher from Norcross, Georgia, said he'd like to try it. So we got hold of some boys who were glad to earn a few nickels, and went out early every morning before the sun got too hot. Reds and I each hit three hundred balls.

We put some pretty big corns on our hands, but outside of that, it didn't hurt us a bit, and we had a lot of fun doing it.

That summer Reds and I were both sold to the St. Louis Cardinals.

Now what has that got to do with selling? Just this: ten years later after I gave up baseball, and had been selling for a couple of years, a big, handsome Southerner named Fred Hagen, was transferred from our company's Atlanta office, to Philadelphia. Fred had a million-dollar smile and personality, but all his selling experience had been among Southern farmers, so he had to develop some new sales talks. He began practicing them on me.

It was the same idea I first learned in baseball. I told Fred the story about Jesse Burkett and about "Reds" Wingo and myself hitting three hundred balls. Fred became enthusiastic about the idea and insisted that I deliver *my* talks to him. We kept on giving our talks to each other, until we knew them backwards. I got so that I loved to give them. I wanted to give a sales talk to everybody I met! Result?

I began making more calls. When a salesman stops making enough calls, frequently the real reason is that he has lost interest and enthusiasm for his own sales story.

A newspaper man called backstage one night to interview John Barrymore after his fifty-sixth performance of Hamlet. The reporter had to wait an hour and a half until after rehearsal. When the great actor finally appeared, the reporter said: "Mr. Barrymore, I'm surprised that you would need a rehearsal after fifty-six performances on Broadway. Why, you're being acclaimed the greatest Hamlet of all time and a genius of the stage!" Barrymore bent over laughing. "Listen," he said. "Do you want to know the truth? For five months, nine hours every day, I read, re-read, studied, and recited that part. I thought I'd never get it into my head. Several times I wanted to quit. I thought I'd missed my calling, and that it was a mistake for me ever to have gone into acting. Yes, a year ago, I wanted to *quit,* and now they are calling me a genius. Isn't that ridiculous?"

I was in a slump at the time I read that story. It prompted me to ask our manager to let me give a sales demonstration before our agency. From the way he looked, I guess he'd never had anyone ask for it before. That put me on the spot, so I rehearsed it, and rehearsed, and rehearsed. As my talk improved, I put more punch into it. I got more excited about it. While I was trying to perfect it, a new idea came to me for the close. Shortly after I gave the demonstration, I closed a large sale that I know I wouldn't have made if I hadn't gone through all those rehearsals. Every time I have been asked to dramatize a sales interview before any group,

I have benefited more—far more, probably—than my audience. Pride, I suppose, drives me to prepare and rehearse until I know I'm ready.

Not long before his death, Knute Rockne, famous football coach of Notre Dame, made a talk to one of the largest sales organizations in the country. It is one of the most practical and inspiring messages on selling I've ever read. Here is the heart of it:

> At Notre Dame, we have a squad of about three hundred lads—both varsity veterans and newcomers. They keep practicing fundamentals, and keep it up, and keep it up, and keep it up, until these various fundamentals become as natural and subconscious as breathing. Then in the game, they don't have to stop and wonder what to do next when the time comes for quick action. The same principles apply to *selling*, just as well as football. If you want to be a star in the selling game, you've got to have your *fundamentals*—the A B C's of your job, so firmly in your mind, that they are part of you. Know them so well that no matter at what point a prospect breaks away from the path to closing, you can get him back on the track again without either of you consciously realizing what has taken place. You can't develop that perfection by looking in the mirror and congratulating your company for taking you on. You've got to *drill* and *drill* and *drill!*

That's what saved John Barrymore from wanting to quit, and helped him to be acclaimed the greatest Hamlet of his day.

That's what raised Jesse Burkett from a weak hitter, and made him one of baseball's immortals! Down to this very day only *four* players have been able to achieve the record of batting over .400 more than one season—Ty Cobb, Rogers Hornsby, Lajoie and Burkett.

Yes, that's what helped *me* get out of the minors and put me in the majors in baseball, and in selling.

SUMMED UP

1. The best time to prepare a speech is immediately after you've made one; likewise a salestalk. All the things you should have said, and should not have said, are fresh in your mind. Write them down *immediately!*

2. Write your talk out word for word. Keep on improving it. Read it and reread it until you know it. But don't memorize it. Try it out on your wife. If it's bad *she'll* tell you. Deliver it to your manager. Deliver it to another salesman. Give it until you love it.

Knute Rockne said it: *"Drill . . . Drill . . . Drill."*

29. HOW TO LET THE CUSTOMER HELP YOU MAKE THE SALE

→» «←

THERE'S an old Chinese proverb that says: "One demonstration is worth more than a thousand words." A good rule, I learned, is never to *say* anything that you can dramatize. Better yet: never dramatize anything yourself that you can get the prospect or customer to do. Let the customer perform. Put him into action. In other words: *Let the customer help you make the sale.*

Let's take a few actual examples of how dramatization was used to help make the sale:

NUMBER 1. General Electric and similar companies had for years been trying to convince school boards of the need for modern lighting in the school rooms. Numerous conferences were held . . . thousands of words. . . . Results? *None!* Suddenly one salesman hit on an idea —dramatization. Standing before the school board in one city, he held a steel rod over his head. Grasping each end with his hands, he bent the rod slightly, as he said: "Gentlemen, I can bend this rod just so far, and it snaps right back (*allowing the rod to straighten out*) but if I bend it beyond a certain point, the rod becomes damaged, and will never straighten out again" (*as he*

210

bent the rod beyond its point of elasticity it snapped slightly in the middle, losing its flexibility). "So it is with the eyes of your little children in the schoolrooms. Their eyes will stand just so much strain. Beyond that, their vision is *permanently* impaired!"

Result? Money was raised. Modern lighting installed immediately!

NUMBER 2. Let's see how a simple little thing like an old-fashioned match was effectively used to dramatize one of the most important selling points of a nationally known refrigerator: Holding a burning match before the customer, the salesman said: "Mrs. Hootnanny, our refrigerator is absolutely silent . . . it is as noiseless as this burning match."

NUMBER 3. Most salesman find it necessary from time to time to submit figures to customers. I've found it far more effective when I can get the customer to do the figuring. I just say: "Mr. Henze, will you write these figures down as I give them to you?" I find it gains better attention; holds his interest; he's less apt to become distracted. It is his own idea at the time! He understands better. He convinces himself with his own figures. In other words, it puts him into action. Later on, coming down to the close, I get him to do the summarizing. I again say, "Mr. Henze, will you write these down?" Then I repeat the summary in fewer words: Number one. . . . Number two. . . . Number three. . . . Number four. . . . It is a natural climax. He is helping to close the sale *himself!*

NUMBER 4. During a drugstore skit I was giving one night in a sales school in Portland, Oregon, a wholesale distributor of woolen cloth saw me dramatize to a "customer" a new type of toothbrush. Placing a large magnifying glass in the customer's hand, I handed him the ordinary type of toothbrush, and also the *new* type. Then I said: "Look at those brushes under the glass, and notice the difference." This cloth salesman had been losing out to competitors who handled a cheaper grade of cloth; he had been unable to convince customers that good quality was good economy. So he decided to try using a pocket magnifying glass in the same way I had used it to dramatize toothbrushes. "I was astonished," he told me later, "how readily the customers recognized the difference. My sales increased immediately."

NUMBER 5. A New York City haberdasher told me he increased his sales of men's clothing 40 per cent when he installed a movie in his store window. The movie dramatized a shabbily dressed man applying for a position, and getting a fast brush-off. The next applicant, well-groomed, got the job quickly. *Good clothes are a good investment* ended the movie.

NUMBER 6. My friend, Dr. Oliver R. Campbell, Aldine Trust Building, Philadelphia, one of the outstanding dentists of Philadelphia, recognizes the value of dramatization. He takes X-ray pictures of his patients' teeth and projects them onto the wall of his office. His patient sits there and watches a movie of his own teeth and gums. Dr. Campbell said he used to wear himself out trying to convince patients of the wisdom of taking care of their teeth before it was too late. After he began to dramatize, he got action.

NUMBER 7. Here's a demonstration I use in my business that

gets action. I use it to dramatize statistics, and have found it impressive with wealthy men. I lay a black fountain pen on a man's desk directly in front of him, place a shiny quarter-dollar alongside the pen, and a dime on the opposite side of it. Then I ask: "Do you know what that is?" The man will generally answer, "No, what is it?" I smile and say: "The pen is *you* when you die; the quarter represents what you have now; the dime shows all that is left for your wife and children when your executors get through paying taxes and other costs." Then I say: "Mr. Mehrer, let me ask you one question. Let's suppose for a few minutes you passed out of the picture last month. You and I are the executors. We have got to convert three-fifths of the estate into cash to meet these taxes. How are we going to do it?" Then I let *him* talk!

Rapid strides have been made in dramatization in recent years. It is a sure-fire method for selling your ideas. Are you making the most of it?

SUMMED UP

"One demonstration is worth more than a thousand words." If possible, let the customer perform the demonstration. Let the customer help you make the sale.

30. HOW I FIND NEW CUSTOMERS AND MAKE OLD ONES ENTHUSI-ASTIC BOOSTERS

⊢⟩⟩⟩ ⟨⟨⟨⊣

THE OTHER day, I tried to figure up how many automobiles I have bought in my time. I was surprised to find that I had bought approximately thirty-three cars.

Now let me ask you a question: How many different salesmen would you guess sold me those thirty-three automobiles? Exactly thirty-three. Isn't that amazing? Not one of those salesmen ever once, to my knowledge, made an attempt to get in touch with me again. Those fellows who seemed so much interested in me before I bought, never so much as picked up the phone and called me to find out if everything was all right. As soon as I paid my money and they collected their commission, they seemed to suddenly vanish from the face of the earth.

Is that unusual? Listen, I have asked more than fifteen thousand people in audiences all over the country if anyone ever had that same experience, and more than half of them promptly raised their hands.

Does that prove that selling automobiles is different from other lines of selling? Does it pay the automobile salesman better to forget the customer, and devote all his time to looking for new buyers? Well, here is the motto one large sales organization has given to its salesmen: *Never forget a customer; never let a customer forget you.*

You guessed it. That is an automobile sales organization. The Chevrolet Motor Company. Adopting this for their motto, they raised themselves to first place in sales compared with all the other automobile manufacturers in the world, and stayed there for thirteen years out of the last fifteen years, for which figures are available.

LOVE.HIS PROPERTY

I guess I'm safe in saying that everybody who buys anything likes courtesy, attention, and service. So we won't waste time discussing that. Let's be frank, and consider it entirely from the selfish viewpoint.

Looking back over my own career of selling, the biggest regret I have is that I didn't spend *twice* as much time calling on, studying and servicing my customers' interests. I mean that literally and sincerely. I could give a hundred examples right out of my records why it would have paid me much more financially, with less nervous strain, less physical effort—and greater happiness.

Yes, sir, if I had my whole career to live over again, I would adopt as my motto and hang it up on the wall over my desk: *Never forget a customer; never let a customer forget you.*

Years ago I bought a rather large home. I liked the place immensely, but it cost so much that after I closed the deal I wondered whether I had made a mistake. So I began to worry. Two or three weeks after we moved into the new home, the real estate broker called me on the phone and said he'd like to see me. It was on a Saturday morning. When he arrived, I was curious. Well, he sat down and congratulated me on my wisdom in selecting that property. Then he told me many things about the place and some interesting history of the surrounding countryside. Later he took me for a walk all around that section, pointed out different lovely homes and told me the names of the owners. Some of them were rather prominent people. He made me feel proud. That salesman showed even *more* enthusiasm and love for my property than he had when he was trying to sell it to me. But he couldn't possibly have been too enthusiastic about the place then, because he was talking about *my property*.

His visit reassured me that I had not made a mistake, and he made me happy. I felt grateful to him. In fact, that morning I formed a strong liking for that man. Our relationship became more than buyer and seller. We became friends.

This cost him an entire Saturday morning when he could have been out seeing a new prospect. However, about a week later, I called him up and gave him the name of a close friend of mine who showed an interest in a property near mine. My friend didn't buy that property, but in a short time this broker located just the right place for him and a good sale resulted.

One evening, in St. Petersburg, Florida, I spoke on this subject. The following night, one of the men in the audience came to me and told me this story:

"This morning, a little elderly lady came into our store and looked at a beautiful diamond brooch. Finally, she bought it, and wrote out a check. While I was wrapping the box, I thought of what you said about 'loving *his* property.' As I handed the package to her, I began making more fuss over the pin than I had when I was selling it to her. I told her how much I loved that pin. I told her the diamond was one of the finest we had ever had in our store, that it had come from the largest and one of the finest diamond mines in the world in South Africa, and that I hoped she would live a great many years to wear it and enjoy it.

"Do you know, Mr. Bettger," he said, "tears filled her eyes, and she said I had made her so happy—because she had started to worry, and wonder whether she hadn't been foolish to spend so much money on herself for a piece of jewelry. I walked out to the front door with her, thanked her sincerely, and asked if she wouldn't stop in and see us any time. Within one hour that little old lady came back with another elderly lady who was stopping at the same hotel. She introduced me to her friend as though I were her own son and asked me to show them around the store. The second lady didn't buy anything as expensive as the first one but she *did* make a purchase. And when I left them at the front door, I knew I had made two good new friends."

You never know when someone is taking your measure. Years ago a plainly dressed little old lady walked into a department store. The other clerks paid no attention to her but one young clerk not only waited on her courteously but carried her packages out to the front door. Seeing that it was raining, he raised her umbrella, took her arm, and walked her to the the corner where he helped her on a trolley car. A few days later, a letter was received by the head of the store, from Andrew Carnegie, thanking them for the courtesy extended to his mother. And he gave them an order for the furnishing of a new home he had just built.

Would you be interested to know what became of that young clerk, who had that kind of feeling for a customer? That salesclerk today is the head of a great department store in a large Eastern city.

Some time ago, I asked Mr. J. J. Pocock, 1817 Chestnut Street, Philadelphia, one of the country's largest distributors of Frigidaires: "What is your best source of new business?" Mr. Pocock answered my question with one word: "Users." Then he added something with a significant emphasis that I'll never forget. And he backed it up with facts so motivating, I found myself out the very next day to see if it would work for me. It worked like magic. It always works. It just can't miss! Here is what Mr. Pocock said:

"New customers are the best source of new business. New customers!"

I asked him why? He said: "New customers are enthusiastic and happy about their new purchase, especially a new convenience they are using. Usually they are excited about it, and proud. They are anxious to tell their friends and neighbors about it. Our salesmen make courtesy calls a week or so after installation of all our electrical products. He finds out whether the new user is getting along all right with her new refrigerator, or whatever it is. He makes suggestions, and offers help or service. You can get more good prospects from these new users than from anyone else."

Mr. Pocock told me about surveys his company made in various parts of the country. The results were consistently the same. For example, in one typical Midwestern city, out of 55 new buyers who were questioned, it was found that the salesmen had made courtesy calls on only 17. Eight out of the 17 gave the salesmen names of prospects whom they called on and sold $1,500 worth of business. Just being courteous immediately produced $1,500 worth of new business. But listen to this: If *all 55 new owners* had been followed up promptly, what would have happened? Figure it up: $1,500 \div 17$ calls $= $90 per call. $90 \times 55 = $4,900!

Mr. Pocock said: "Experience has taught us this lesson: *When you sell 'em, don't forget 'em!*"

Here is another significant fact he told me: "Over half of the buyers we question tell us that a friend or relative first interested them in buying."

The last thing Mr. Pocock said to me was: "If you take care of your customers, they'll take care of you."

For many years I have carried a letter around in my pocket. It seldom fails to produce one or more leads wherever I use it. With a little alteration, perhaps you may be able to use it.

Mr. William R. Jones
Real Estate Trust Building
Philadelphia, Pa.
Dear Bill:
    I want you to know Frank Bettger. In my opin-

ion, he is one of the best qualified life insurance men in Philadelphia. I have given him my entire confidence, and I have acted on his suggestions.

Maybe you have not been thinking about life insurance, but I know that it will pay you to listen to Mr. Bettger, because he has some very constructive ideas and services which will be of benefit to you and your family.

Sincerely,
Bob

Let me illustrate how I used this letter just recently. I read in the morning newspaper that friends of mine, Murphy, Quigley Company, prominent building contractors, had been awarded a new job. Within twenty minutes, I had Robert Quigley on the phone and made an appointment. As I walked into Mr. Quigley's private office, it was easy to give him a big, glad smile: "Congratulations, Bob!"

As I shook his hand, he asked: "What about?"

I said: "I just read in this morning's *Inquirer* about your being awarded the contract for the new addition to the U.G.I. Building."

"Oh, thanks," he smiled. Was he pleased? How could he help but be pleased? I asked him to tell me all about it. Then I listened!

Finally, I said: "Look, Bob, in preparing your bid, you probably asked for bids from several sub-contractors, didn't you?"

"Sure," he replied.

Out came my letter of introduction. Handing the letter to him, I said: "Bob, you've probably already promised the job to some of these sub-contractors who gave you low bids, isn't that right?"

Grinning, he said: "Yes, a couple of them."

As he finished reading the letter, he asked: "What do you want me to do, write this letter on one of our letterheads to some of these fellows?"

I walked out of that office with four letters of introduction to plumbing, heating, electrical, and painting contractors.

It's not always convenient for a man to give me a letter of introduction, so I carry with me a 4" x 2½" card that reads like this:

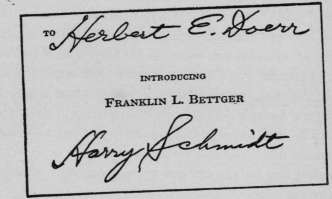

TO *Herbert E. Doerr*

INTRODUCING

FRANKLIN L. BETTGER

Harry Schmidt

My friend writes on the upper part of the card the name of the prospect, then signs his name at the bottom of the card.

If he hesitates, I say: "Look, if your friend were here right now, you wouldn't hesitate to introduce me, would you?"

Usually he says: "No, of course not." Then he fills out the card. Sometimes he'll give me several.

Occasionally men refuse to give me the name of anybody. About a year ago, a hard-boiled client of mine answered me like this: "I wouldn't send you to see my worst enemy!"

I asked: "Why?"

He said: "Look here, Bettger, I *hate* insurance men. I hate to see them come in here. If one ever walked in here, and told me that one of my friends sent him, I'd be sore as hell! And I'd call up the guy who sent him and tell him so. Anything else but an insurance man, I wouldn't mind!"

This really was being brutally frank. But I managed to smile, and said: "That's all right, Mr. Blank, I think I understand how you feel. I'll tell you what I'll do. Give me the name of someone you know, under fifty, who is making money. I promise you I'll *never* mention your name to him.

"Well," he said, "on that basis, if you can find a way to get in to see Carroll Zeigler, surgical instrument manufacturer, 918 N. 19th Street, he's about forty-one years old, and very successful."

I thanked him for the tip, and again promised I wouldn't use his name.

I drove directly over to Mr. Zeigler's plant. As I walked in, I said: "Mr. Zeigler, my name is Bettger. I'm in the life insurance business. A mutual friend gave me your name with the understanding that I wouldn't mention his name. He told me that you have been very successful, and that you should be a good man for me to talk to. Could you spare me five minutes now, or would you rather I stop some other time?"

"What did you want to talk to me about?" he asked.

"*You,*" was my answer.

"What about me? If it's insurance you want to talk about, I'm not interested."

"That's perfectly all right, Mr. Zeigler," I said, "I don't want to talk to you about insurance today. May I have just five minutes?"

He held me down to exactly five minutes. In that time, I was able to get from him all the information I needed.

I have sold Mr. Zeigler three times since then, totaling a very substantial amount of business. Here's a strange thing: We have become good friends, yet never once has he asked who sent me to him.

Which is the best time to follow a referred lead? Within six days? Or six weeks? Six minutes I've found best, or just as soon as it is possible for me to get there. A new lead is sizzling hot! If I don't go immediately, while I'm steamed up about it, it gets pushed back somewhere in my files and I lose interest in it. When I get it out of the file at a later date, it's just like one of my company's best young salesmen, John Lord, says: "It looks like a stale loaf of bread."

We never know what is back of one of these leads. Many times the friend who gives the lead is familiar with some timely situation which he is not at liberty to disclose.

APPRECIATION

Here is a courtesy which I have found equally as important as procuring the name itself. Whatever happens, good or bad, I always report back to the friend who had the confidence in me to give me the lead. Failure to report back is sure to offend a man. He may never mention it, but he may always hold it against you. I know. I have been on both ends, and I have felt that unfavorable reaction both as giver and receiver of a recommendation.

Furthermore, when I report back that I've made a sale, and show how grateful I feel, my friend seems just as happy about it as I am. If I am not successful in making a sale, I report back, and tell exactly what happened. It's surprising how frequently he'll dig up another lead that is better.

I had lunch recently with the president of a large bank in a Western city. He gave me a copy of the type of letter which they have found most effective in expressing appreciation to their customers who introduce friends to their bank:

> Dear Mr. Brown:
> I want you to know how greatly we appreciate your bringing Mr. Smith to our bank. The spirit of friendliness and cooperation which you have shown by introducing Mr. Smith and other friends to the First National Bank has been a source of a great deal of pleasure to us. You will always find us eager to render the kind of service you would like to have us give you and your friends.
> Sincerely yours,

Many years ago, I had the great thrill of seeing Willie Hoppe win the world's billiard championship. I was surprised how much time he spent studying some simple little shots that even I could have made. I soon found out it wasn't those easy shots he was studying; he was thinking about how he was going to play position for the next shot and perhaps the next dozen shots. Hoppe's opponent seemed to be every bit as good a shot, but too frequently left himself in a poor position for the next shot.

Now I can understand better how it was possible for him to set up that unbelievable world's record of running more than 15 million points in billiards. Forty-three years a title-holder. Try to match that record in any other sport!

The big lesson I learned from Willie Hoppe that night, which has always remained fresh in my mind, is this: *It is just as important to play position for the next shot in selling, as it is in billiards.* In fact, it is the life-blood of our business!

I heard Robert B. Coolidge, vice-president of the Aetna Life Insurance Company of Hartford, Connecticut, put it this way: "Prospecting is like shaving... if you don't do something about it every day, first thing you know, you'll be a bum."

SUMMED UP

1. "Never forget a customer; never let a customer forget you."

2. "If you take care of your customers, they'll take care of you."

3. Love *HIS* Property.

4. New customers are the best source of new business . . . *new* customers!

5. When is the best time to follow a referred lead? Within six days . . . or six weeks? . . . Six *minutes,* I found *best.*

6. Never fail to show appreciation for a lead. Report results whether good or bad.

7. Play position for the next shot.

31. SEVEN RULES I USE IN CLOSING THE SALE

❧❧❧   ❧❧❧

Y OU WILL recall how I became so discouraged that I
think I would have quit, if I hadn't got the idea, one
Saturday morning, of trying to get at the root of my
worries.

First I asked myself: *"Just what is the problem?"* It was
this: I was not getting high enough returns for the stagger-
ing number of calls I was making. I did well at selling a
prospect, until the moment came for closing the sale. Then
the customer would say: "Well, I'll think it over, Mr. Bettger. Come and see me again." It was the time I wasted on
follow-up calls that was causing my depression.

Second I asked myself: *"What are the possible solutions?"*
For the answer, I got out my record book for the last twelve
months and studied facts. I made an astounding discovery!
Seventy per cent of my sales had been closed on the first interview. Twenty-three per cent had been closed on the
second interview. And only seven per cent on the third,
fourth, fifth, etc., interviews. In other words, I was wasting
one-half my working day on business which paid only seven
per cent. The answer was obvious. Immediately I cut out

all visits beyond the second interview, and spent the extra time building up new prospects. The results were unbelievable. Soon I had raised the cash value of every visit from $2.80 to $4.27 a call.

Now would this same conclusion work out in every line of selling? You probably have already answered that one. Let me give you one example. For two years a large industrial concern made a study of reports turned in by their entire sales force. They were astonished to find that 75 per cent of the business produced by their salesmen was sold *after* the fifth interview! But listen to this: they also discovered that 83 per cent of their lower-bracket salesmen quit calling on prospects whom they failed to sell *before* the fifth interview!

What does this prove? It proves again the importance of keeping complete records, and studying them regularly. The enormous value to both the salesman *and* the company has been demonstrated so often that I wonder why every sales executive doesn't make it *absolutely compulsory*.

Although the discovery I made enabled me to double my income by eliminating all visits beyond the second interview, the figures also showed that I was closing only one out of twelve. I still didn't know how to bring people to a decision.

Then one night shortly afterward I had the good fortune to hear Dr. Russell H. Conwell, founder of Temple University, speak at the Central Y.M.C.A., in Philadelphia. His subject was "The Four Rules for a Good Speech." Coming down to the close of his inspiring talk, Dr. Conwell said: "Number Four. Appeal for Action! Here is where so many otherwise good speakers fall down. They win their cause with the world at large, but fail to win the support of their audience. They have amused it, they have entertained it; but they haven't *sold* it anything. It has afforded the most thrilling basis for climax since public speaking began . . ."

Appeal for Action! That was where I had been falling down. I began to read everything I could find on the subject of closing the sale. I found that probably more had been written about it than any other step in the sale. I talked with top-notch salesmen and found out what they had to say about appealing for action. Out of all this, and other things which grew out of my own experience, here are the seven outstanding rules that have been responsible for the progress I was able to make in bringing people to a decision:

1. SAVE CLOSING POINTS FOR THE CLOSE

In my eagerness to sell, I had been using closing points too early in the interview. I learned that the average successful sale goes through *four* steps: (1) Attention, (2) Interest, (3) Desire, (4) Close.

When I began holding my closing points back for the close, it enabled the prospect to judge my plan with an open mind. It avoided building up so much sales resistance. Then when it came time for action, I had something to get excited about! My punch lines went over better; they had more power in them. Instead of forcing myself to be enthusiastic, I sometimes had to suppress my excitement. And I found that *suppressed excitement* is most effective in arousing the prospect's enthusiasm at the close of the sale.

2. SUMMARIZE

I discovered that a good summary affords the best basis for climax in selling. How long should the summary be? A superb test is used by one great sales manager. He compels each one of his salesmen to summarize the advantages of his product while holding a burning match. In any event a summary should be brief.

I find it even more effective when I can get the buyer to summarize. It puts him into action. I say: "Will you write these down?" Then I repeat the summary in fewer words: "Number One . . . Number Two . . . Number Three . . . Number Four . . ." It is a natural climax where you have the buyer keeping in step with you, right down to where he will be helping to close the sale himself.

3. A MAGIC PHRASE

After presenting the plan, and summarizing it, I look at the prospect and ask: "How do you like it?"

It is surprising how frequently he answers: "I think I like it." I assume this means he is going to buy so I don't wait another moment. I begin to ask the necessary questions and write his answers on the application form. I always begin with unimportant questions. Once he starts giving me the answers, he seldom balks. When there are alternatives in the plan, I get him to choose between them.

I believe it is important to mention here, that during the presentation, I try to get a couple of "yes's" from the prospect. For example, after showing him a good feature, I say: "Don't you think that's a good idea?" Usually he will nod and say "Yes."

4. WELCOME OBJECTIONS

It took me a long time to understand that the best prospects are the ones who object. I was surprised when I learned that many of the objections which had been getting rid of me were really buying signals. For example: "I can't afford it. . . . See me in January. . . . See me in the spring. . . . I want to think it over. . . . I want to talk it over with my wife. . . . Your price is too high. I can do better than that."

I learned that objections like these are *not* turn-downs. Example: If the objection is: "I can't afford it," he really is telling me he *wants* it. So the only problem then is to show him how he can pay for it. People seldom resent a salesman's being persistent and forceful, if he is talking in terms of their interest. In fact, he is admired and respected more for it.

5. WHY? . . . IN ADDITION TO THAT . . . ?

I must come back again to the phrase: "In addition to that." I try to hold this question back as my final ace in the hole. I use "why?" all through the interview in different forms. I may not always use the word itself, but I am asking "why?" nevertheless.

Let me give you an example of a sale told to me by one salesman who attended our lecture course in Chattanooga, Tennessee, a few years ago. This salesman had reached that part of the interview where the prospect said: "Well, I won't do anything about it now . . . get in touch with me in the fall—after the fifteenth of September."

"This is where I had been folding up," the salesman told me.

Listen to how he passed the ball back into the prospect's hands in the following sale, the sale of a business-training course:

PROSPECT. . . . See me after September fifteenth.

SALESMAN. Mr. Carroll, if your boss called you into his office tomorrow morning and offered you a raise in pay, you wouldn't say: "No, see me after September fifteenth," would you?

PROSPECT. No, of course not. He'd think I was nuts.

SALESMAN. Well, isn't that practically what you're telling me now? Just write your name here (*pointing to dotted line*) just as it's filled in at the top, and you'll have several lessons completed by September fifteenth.

PROSPECT (*picking up application form*). Leave this and any literature you've got with me. I'll think it over and let you know next week.

SALESMAN. Why don't you sign it now?

PROSPECT. I don't think I should take this course right now.

SALESMAN. Why?

PROSPECT. Well . . . I really can't afford it.

SALESMAN (*pause*) . . . *In addition to that,* isn't there something else in the back of your mind? . . . Isn't there something else holding you back from making this important decision?

PROSPECT. No, that's the only reason. I always seem to be short of money.

SALESMAN. Mr. Carroll, *if you were my own brother, I'd say to you what I'm going to say to you now.*

PROSPECT. What's that?

SALESMAN. Write your name here *now,* and let's get started!

PROSPECT. What's the smallest amount I can pay now, and how much would I have to pay each month?

SALESMAN. You state the amount you can pay now, and I'll let you know whether you can begin.

PROSPECT. Would $25 now and $10 a month be all right?

SALESMAN. It's a deal. Write your name here (x......) and you've made the first step.

PROSPECT (*signs application form*).

6. ASK PROSPECT TO WRITE HIS NAME HERE

 X..

I always have a heavy "X" penciled where the prospect signs. I simply hand him my pen, and pointing to the large X say: "Will you write your name here the same as I have filled it in up at the top?" Whenever possible, I have the application pretty well filled in. At least, I always try to have his name and address at the top.

7. GET CHECK WITH THE ORDER. DON'T BE AFRAID OF MONEY

Records of successful salesmen prove that asking for cash with the order is one of the most powerful factors in closing the sale. The buyer then places a higher value and greater appreciation on your product or service. Once he pays something he feels the product is *his* property. When a prospect has time to review and debate alone, he sometimes decides to postpone action, but I've never had a man cancel an order when he's paid something on account.

THE RIGHT TIME TO CLOSE

When is the right time to close? Sometimes in the first minute. Sometimes not for an hour—or two hours! How do you know when the right time comes to close? Have you ever watched a great fighter in action? Joe Louis was one of the greatest closers who ever climbed through the ropes. I saw Joe close three of his championship fights. The crowd watched him in breathless excitement, because Joe was constantly on the alert testing his opponent, patiently waiting for the right moment. Sometimes that moment appeared right in the first round. Sometimes not for ten or twelve rounds. But Joe quickly followed up each signal for the close. If he found he was mistaken, that master closer resumed his selling job. He knew each attempt would bring him *nearer* to the right moment. Yet he never appeared overanxious.

With years of experience, I found my selling process gradually improving, and I became less and less conscious of any great final effort to close the sale. If my *approach* is right, if I have been able to create sufficient *interest* and *desire*, then, when the time comes for *action*, the prospect is ready and eager to buy.

I have merely attempted, in a very brief way, to explain how I use certain ideas which have been *consistently* helpful to me, things which I believe can be used in every line of selling. For a more complete treatment of the close, I can enthusiastically recommend Charles B. Roth's book, *Secrets of Closing Sales,* published by Prentice-Hall, Inc., New York.

I had these seven things typed on a 3″ x 5″ card and carried it in my pocket for some time. In bold type across the top of the card were these words:

THIS IS GOING TO BE THE
BEST INTERVIEW I EVER HAD

Just before going into a man's office, I repeated those words to myself. It became a habit. And, even to this day, I often find myself repeating them.

The *big* value of the little 3″ x 5″ card, however, was this: after an unsuccessful interview, I checked myself up on the card to see what I had done wrong, or what I might have done differently. That was the acid test!

SUMMARY

POCKET REMINDERS

THIS IS GOING TO BE THE BEST INTERVIEW
I EVER HAD

1. Save closing points for the close. The four steps in the average sale: (1) Attention, (2) Interest, (3) Desire, (4) Close.

2. Summarize. Whenever possible, let the prospect summarize. Put him into *action!*

3. "How Do You Like It?" After concluding the presentation, ask this question. It's magic!

4. Welcome objections! Remember—the best prospects are those who offer objections.

5. "Why? . . . In addition to that?" . . . *Why* gets the customer talking, brings out his objections. *In addition to that?* finds the *real* reason, or the key issue.

6. Ask Prospect to Write His Name Here.

       X...........................

Get application or order blank out early. Try to at least have his name already filled in at the top. You will never know whether you could have closed the sale unless you actually tried to get the order signed.

7. Get check with the order. *Don't be afraid of money.* Successful salesmen say asking for money is one of the most powerful factors in closing the sale.

Check yourself *every day* on these closing rules. Apply them until they become habits.

32. AN AMAZING CLOSING TECHNIQUE I LEARNED FROM A MASTER SALESMAN

EDITOR'S NOTE: *(What do you say to a prospect when you go back for his final decision? Mr. Bettger reveals an extraordinary technique which has enabled him to close many sales.)*

→》》   《《←

IN 1924 I learned an amazing closing technique from a great salesman named Ernest Wilkes. At the time of his discovery, Mr. Wilkes was carrying a debit for the Metropolitan Life Insurance Company in San Francisco, California, collecting ten- and fifteen-cent weekly premiums from industrial policy-holders. As a salesman he rated low. His small salary and commissions just about fed and clothed his wife and children, leaving nothing for himself. His clothes were shabby and poor-fitting; his coat and shirt sleeves badly frayed.

Wilkes' principal difficulty in selling, he told me, was that he'd shoot the works on the first interview, and wind up with the prospect telling him: "Leave this information with me, and I'll think it over. See me again next week."

"When I saw him again," Wilkes said, "I never knew what to say because I had told him everything in the first interview. The answer was always the same: 'Well, Mr. Wilkes,

I've thought it all over and I can't do anything now . . . let it go till next year.'

"Then one day, I hit upon an idea," related Wilkes excitedly. "It worked like magic! I began to close them when I went back for this second interview!"

As I listened to him explain his method it didn't sound right to me. However, I made up my mind to try it. The following morning, I called on a builder named William Eliason, in the Land Title and Trust Building, Philadelphia. Ten days previously, I had presented a plan to Mr. Eliason, and he had said: "Leave this with me, and see me in about two weeks. I'm also considering plans submitted by two other companies."

I followed Mr. Wilkes' instructions precisely. Here's what happened: first I wrote up the application before making the call, filling in all the information I had, such as name in full, business and home address, also the amount of insurance which he said he was considering. Then I placed a large X on the dotted line where the applicant signs.

Wilkes had made an important point of this "X."

X..
Applicant Sign Here

As I entered the outer office the door of Mr. Eliason's private office was open. He was seated at his desk. The receptionist wasn't there at the time. He looked out and recognized me. Shaking his head "no," he waved his hand "goodbye!"

Bent on following instructions to the letter, I continued

walking toward my man with a serious face. (This is one time where a smile is not in order.) Mr. Eliason said in a stern tone: "No. I'm not going to do anything. I've decided to drop the matter. I might take it up again six months from now."

As he spoke, I deliberately removed the application from my pocket, and unfolded it, continuing to walk toward him. Arriving at his side, I laid it on his desk, directly in front of him.

Then I spoke the first words Wilkes told me to say: "Is that right, Mr. Eliason?"

As he read I removed my fountain pen from my vest pocket, adjusted it for writing, but stood there quietly. I was actually scared. This all seemed wrong.

Presently he looked up: "What is this, an application?"

"No," was the answer.

"Why it certainly is! It says 'application' right up here at the top," he pointed.

"It won't be an application until you write your name here," I said. (As I spoke, I handed the open pen to him, and touched one finger on the dotted line.)

He did exactly as Wilkes said he would do—took the pen from my hand without seeming to be conscious of taking it! More silence while he read. Finally getting up from his chair he walked slowly over to the window and leaned against the wall. He must have read every word on that paper. All this time there was absolute silence. Five minutes must have passed before he returned to his desk, sat down, and began to sign his name with my pen. As he wrote, he said: "I guess I'd better sign this. If I don't, I'm afraid I'll die!"

With the greatest effort to control my voice, I managed to say: "Do you want to give me a check for the full year, Mr. Eliason, or would you rather just pay half now, and the balance in six months?"

"How much is it?" he asked.

"Only $432," I replied.

Pulling his checkbook out of a drawer, he took a look and said, "Oh well, I'd better pay it all now; if I don't I'll be just as broke six months from now."

When he handed me the check, and my fountain pen, it seemed all I could do to keep from letting out a great yell! The miracle close that Ernest Wilkes discovered, and which sounded so unnatural, proved to be a natural!

I've never had anyone get angry with me for trying it. And when it fails, it never stops me from going back later to try to complete the sale.

Just what is the psychology back of this thing? I don't know. Perhaps it is this: you keep a man's mind concentrating on *signing*—not on refusing. You finally crowd out all the reason why he shouldn't, until his mind just keeps subconsciously thinking of all those reasons why he should. All thoughts tend to pass into action.

If your prospect clearly understands your proposition, and you believe it is to his best interest to act—why start from scratch in the second interview? Why not put the ball down on the one-yard line? What generally happens when one team gets the other team down on the one-yard line? A touchdown! Isn't that right? A touchdown! The team with the ball reaches a high state of excitement and feels they can't be stopped. They expect to score; and they usually do. Their opponents are on the defense. They are on the run. Momentum sweeps them over the line.

While this close is primarily to be used in the final interview, I believe many times the sale is made right in the first interview but we don't realize it. Often, by using this technique, I've been able to close sales on the first interview that I had been walking away from previously.

Here is a strange experience. After I had been using this idea for nearly three years, I had an offer made to me by a large financial institution. It was a rather flattering one. At the end of the first interview, it was agreed that I should think it over, and a second appointment was set for ten days later. During that time, I talked it over with several friends, older men with long experience. My decision finally was to turn the offer down.

As I was ushered into an attractive office ten days later by an official of the company, *there was my contract lying on his desk, directly in front of me as I sat down.* It was completely drawn up in my name; there was a beautiful gold seal at the bottom and an "X" on the dotted line where I was to sign!

I read it quietly for some time.

Not a word was spoken.

All the reasons why I'd decided *not* to accept their offer suddenly vanished from my mind. All the reasons why I *should* accept began racing through my head . . . "the salary was very good; I could absolutely count on it, sick or well, good times or bad . . . it was a great company to be associated with . . ."

When I looked up and began telling this official that I had decided not to accept their offer, and my reasons, it seemed like I was just repeating memorized lines that I really didn't mean. But, to my surprise, he quit cold! He reached out his hand, shook mine warmly, and said: "I'm sorry, Mr. Bettger, we would have liked to have you with us, but I wish you all the luck in the world, and I hope you will be very happy and successful."

The strange thing about the interview was that it never occurred to me, until I left his office, that this man had used the *very same technique* I had been using for three years, yet I was not aware of it while it was going on! Yes, it is a natural. I even had his pen in my hand, but didn't remember his handing it to me! He would have been amazed if he had known how close I was to signing that contract. If he had not quit on the first attempt, if he had stayed with me a little longer . . . *I would have signed.*

By the way, would you be interested to know what happened to Ernest Wilkes, the once poor, shabbily dressed, industrial insurance agent who discovered this idea for closing sales?

Ernest Wilkes became vice-president of the largest corporation in the world—the Metropolitan Life Insurance Company. At the time of his untimely death in 1942, he was generally regarded as next in line for the presidency of that great company.

SUMMARY OF THE STEPS IN
THIS CLOSE
AND
"POCKET REMINDER"

1. Write up the order blank, application, or contract, *in advance,* even though you may only have the prospect's name and address to put on it.

2. Mark a *heavy* "X" each place where he is to sign, if his signature is required.

3. Your first words: "Is that right, Mr. Blank?" laying the paper on his desk directly in front of him. If it is a standing up interview place the unfolded paper in his hands.

4. The ball is now down on his one-yard line. Momentum is with *you!* One of the greatest services one man can render another is to help him come to an intelligent decision.

SUMMARY

PART FIVE

POCKET REMINDERS

1. Don't try to throw the *hawser*—throw the *heaving line*. The approach must have only one objective—selling the sales interview. Not your product—your *interview*. It is the sale before the sale.

2. The foundation of sales lies in getting interviews. And the secret of getting good, attentive, courteous interviews is in selling appointments! The secret of making appointments is to stop swinging for a *home run,* and merely try to get on *first base*. First, sell the appointment. Second, sell your product.

3. The best way to outsmart secretaries and switchboard operators is never to try! Be honest and sincere with them. Take them into your confidence. Never use trickery or subterfuge.

4. "If you want to be a *star* in the selling game, you've got to have your fundamentals—the ABC's of your job—so firmly in your mind, that they are part of you. . . ." Write your sales talk out word for word. Keep on improving it. Read it and reread it until you know it. But don't memorize it. Try it out on your wife, your manager, another salesman. Give it until you love it. Knute Rockne said it: *"Drill . . . Drill . . . Drill."*

5. Make the most of dramatization. "One demonstration is worth more than a thousand words." Let the customer perform. *Let the customer help you make the sale.*

6. "Never forget a customer; never let a customer forget you." New customers are the best source of new business . . . *new* customers! Follow up referred leads while they are sizzling hot. Report results— whether good or bad. *Play position for the next shot.*

7. Check yourself *each day* on the rules for closing the sale. Apply them until they become as natural as breathing. Review

"Pocket Reminders" pages 237 and 245 after an unsuccessful interview, to see what you have done wrong, or what you might have done differently. That is the acid test.

Part Six

DON'T BE AFRAID TO FAIL

≫ ≪

33. DON'T BE AFRAID TO FAIL!

→≫ ≪←

IT WAS a beautiful Saturday afternoon in the summer of 1927, and thirty-five thousand wildly excited baseball fans packed Shibe Park, Philadelphia. They were giving Babe Ruth the "razzberry"—and good! Bob Grove, one of the greatest left-handed pitchers of all time, had just struck Babe Ruth out on three pitched balls for the second successive time. Two runners were on the bases.

As the great slugger returned to the bench amidst wild and abusive jeering, he looked up into the stands with an unruffled smile, just as he did the first time, gave his cap a polite little tip from his perspiring brow, stepped down into the dugout and calmly took his drink of water.

In the eighth inning when he came up for his third turn at bat, the situation was critical. The Athletics were leading the Yankees, 3 to 1. The bases were full and two were out. As Babe selected his favorite bat and started toward the plate, the crowd rose in a body as if by signal. The excitement was tremendous!

"Strike 'im out again!" pleaded the fans to Grove. Strutting around the pitcher's box, it was easy to see that the big southpaw just knew he would.

As the mighty batter took his position, the crowd became hysterical. There was a pause. Mickey Cochrane, the A's great catcher, crouched to give the signal. Grove threw one with lightning speed. Ruth swung—foul tip. "Str—ike one!" roared the umpire. Again the signal, and the pitch—too fast to follow. Again, Babe took that magnificent swing—and missed: "Stri—i-i-ke tuh!" roared the ump.

Ruth staggered—*and went down.* He had literally swung himself off his feet. There was a cloud of dust as the big fellow sprawled on the ground. The crowd was going mad. I turned to a stranger standing alongside of me and shouted something in his ear. But the noise was so great I couldn't even hear my own voice. Finally, regaining his feet, the Bambino brushed the dust off his trousers, dried his hands and got set for the next pitch. Grove delivered the ball so fast none of the fans saw it. Babe swung—but this time he connected! It was only a split second before everybody seemed to realize what had happened. That ball was never coming back again!

It disappeared over the scoreboard and cleared the houses across the street—one of the longest hits ever made in baseball.

As Babe Ruth trotted around the bases and across the plate behind the other runners—with what proved to be the winning run—he received a wild ovation from the crowd.

I watched Ruth closely as he looked up into the stands and doffed his cap with that little smile, and *the expression on his face was exactly like the one he wore on his first two trips, when he had taken the razzing.*

Later in the season, after the Yanks clinched the American League pennant, Grantland Rice interviewed Ruth. "Babe," he asked, "what do you do when you get in a batting slump?" Babe replied: "I just keep goin' up there and keep swingin' at 'em. I know the old law of averages will hold good for me the same as it does for anybody else, if I keep havin' my healthy swings. If I strike out two or three times in a game, or fail to get a hit for a week, why should I worry? Let the pitchers worry; they're the guys who're gonna suffer later on."

This unshakable faith in making the law of averages work for him enabled Babe Ruth to accept his bad breaks and failures with a smile. This simple philosophy had much to do with making him baseball's greatest slugger. His attitude of taking both good and bad in stride made him one of the game's greatest showmen, biggest box-office attractions, and the highest paid player of all time.

Why is it, when we read about the great achievements of successful men in sports, or business, we are seldom told about their failures? For example: we now read of the amazing record of the immortal Babe Ruth, with his unapproached total of 851 home runs, but another unapproached world's record of his is carefully buried in the records, never to be mentioned—*striking out more times than any other player in history.* He *failed* 1,330 times! One thousand three hundred and thirty times he suffered the humiliation of walking back to the bench amidst jeers and ridicule. But he never allowed fear of failure to slow him down or weaken his effort. When he struck out he didn't count that failure —that was effort!

Are you discouraged by your failures? Listen! Your average may be as good as anybody's. If you fail to find your name on the list of makers-good, don't blame it on your failures. Examine your records. You'll probably discover the real reason is lack of effort. Not enough exposure. You don't give old man law of averages sufficient chance to work for you.

Study this average: in 1915 Ty Cobb set up the astonishing all-time record of stealing 96 bases. In 1922, seven years later, Max Carey of the Pittsburgh Pirates set the second-best record, 51 stolen bases. Does this mean that Cobb was twice as good as Carey, his closest rival? I'll let you decide.

Here are the facts:

	Cobb	Carey
Attempts	134	53
Failed	38	2
Succeeded	96	51
Average	71%	96%

We find that Carey's average was much better than Cobb's but Cobb tried 81 more times than Carey. His 81 tries produced 44 more stolen bases. He risked failure 81 more times in one season than his closest rival. Cobb goes down in history as the greatest base-runner of all time. He is generally regarded as the greatest player of all time.

Ty Cobb refused to fear failure. Did it pay him? Well, Ty has been able to live quite comfortably in retirement for eighteen years and deems it wise to pay premiums each year on a large amount of life insurance so that the executors of his estate will have enough cash to pay Uncle Sam the estate taxes.

Do you believe in yourself and the things you want to do? Are you prepared for many setbacks and failures? Whatever your calling may be, each error, each failure is like a strike out. Your greatest asset is the number of strike outs you have had since your last hit. The greater the number, the nearer you are to your next hit.

I was inspired by studying this record of failures:

A young man ran for the legislature in Illinois, and was badly swamped.

He next entered business—failed—and spent seventeen years of his life paying up the debts of a worthless partner.

He was in love with a beautiful young woman to whom he became engaged—then she died.

Re-entering politics, he ran for Congress, and was badly defeated.

He then tried to get an appointment to the United States Land Office—but failed.

He became a candidate for the United States Senate—and was badly defeated.

Two years later he was defeated by Douglas.

One failure after another—bad failures—great setbacks; but in the face of all this, he kept on trying and became one of the greatest men in all history.

Perhaps you've heard of him. His name was Abraham Lincoln.

Recently I met an ex-salesman who is now clerk in a small manufacturing plant. He told me fear of failure had caused him to fail as a salesman. "When I went out on a lead furnished by my company, I was actually glad when my prospect was not in. If he was in, I was so afraid I'd fail to get the order, I would be nervous, overanxious, and unnatural. Consequently, I'd put up a miserable effort to make the sale."

Fear of failure is a weakness which is common to most men, women and children.

I had breakfast the other morning at the Mt. Alto Hotel with Richard W. Campbell, of Altoona, Pennsylvania. Dick has achieved a phenomenal record selling life insurance for the Fidelity Mutual Life Insurance Company. Here is a man who has almost literally lifted himself by his own bootstraps. I asked him if he had ever been bothered with fear of failure. I was surprised when he said it nearly drove him out of selling. Let's listen to Dick for a moment:

"Nobody could get much lower in spirit and more discouraged than I was: couldn't pay my bills—no money—always broke. Yet, the tougher things got, the *fewer* people I called on. I became so ashamed of my reports that I began to pad them with calls I never made—(my own private records) yes, I began to cheat myself. No man can get much lower than that! One day, I drove way out into the country on a lonely road and turned off the ignition. I sat there for three hours. 'Why did you do this?' I asked myself. I put myself through white heat. 'Campbell,' I said to myself, 'if that's the kind of fellow you are—if you're going to be crooked with yourself, you're going to be crooked with the other fellow. You're doomed to failure . . . there's only one choice to make, and the choice must be made by you—and now. No other time will do—it's got to be done *now! ! !*'"

Since that day Dick Campbell has kept complete and accurate records definitizing his work and his plan of living. Dick said, "In this world, we either discipline ourselves, or we are disciplined by the world. I prefer to discipline myself." Dick Campbell believes that adopting this plan enabled him to eliminate all fear of failure. Said he: "Whenever a salesman gets out of the habit of seeing enough prospects, he loses his sense of indifference."

That's what Babe Ruth had—a sense of indifference. Brother Gilbert, who discovered Babe Ruth, said: He looked better striking out than he did hitting home runs."

Dr. Louis E. Bisch, one of the nation's leading psychiatrists, wrote: "Cultivate a little the don't-care habit; don't worry about what people may think. This will endear you to others and make you liked and loved all the more."

When you try too hard and become overanxious, you look bad. You are bad. Yes, keep going, but don't be afraid to lose today. Today is not going to make or break you. You can't bat .300 every day. The crowd loves a good loser; everybody despises a quitter.

"My great concern," said Lincoln, "is not whether you have failed, but whether you are content with your failure."

Thomas Edison had ten thousand failures before he invented the incandescent bulb. Edison made up his mind that each failure brought him that much closer to success.

Nobody will remember the times you struck out in the

early innings if you hit a home run with the bases full in the ninth.

Failures mean nothing at all if success comes eventually. And that's a thought that should cheer you up and help you keep on keeping on when the going seems hard.

Keep going! Each week, each month, you are improving. One day soon, you will find a way to do the thing that today looks impossible.

It was Shakespeare who wrote: "Our doubts are traitors, and make us lose the good we oft might win, by fearing to attempt."

COURAGE IS NOT THE ABSENCE OF FEAR, IT IS THE
CONQUEST OF IT.

34. BENJAMIN FRANKLIN'S SECRET OF SUCCESS AND WHAT IT DID FOR ME

->>>   <<<-

THIS CHAPTER probably should have been in the beginning of the book, but I have saved it for the last, because it is, perhaps, the most important of all. It is the track I ran on.

I was born during the blizzard of 1888 in a little row house on Nassau Street, in Philadelphia. On both sides of our street there were lamp-posts about every fifty yards. As a small boy I can remember watching every evening just about dark for the lamp-lighter who came through the street carrying a roaring torch. He stopped at each lamp-post, reached his torch high up into the lamp and lighted it. I usually watched him until he disappeared from sight, leaving a trail of lights behind him so that people could see their way.

Many years later, when I was groping around in the dark, desperately trying to learn how to sell, I picked up a book that had a tremendous effect on my life, *The Autobiography of Benjamin Franklin*. Franklin's life reminded me of that lamp-lighter. He, too, left a trail of lights behind him so that others could see their way.

One of those lights stood out like a great beacon, an idea discovered by Franklin when he was just a small printer in Philadelphia and badly in debt. He thought of himself as a simple man of ordinary ability, but believed he could acquire the essential principles of successful living, if only he could find the right method. Having an inventive mind, he devised a method so simple, yet so practical, that anyone could use it.

Franklin chose thirteen subjects which he felt were necessary or desirable for him to acquire and try to master, and he gave a week's strict attention to each subject successively. In this way, he was able to go through his entire list in thirteen weeks, and repeat the process four times in a year. You will find an exact duplicate of Franklin's thirteen subjects on page 264 just as they appear in his autobiography.

When he was seventy-nine years old, Benjamin Franklin wrote more about this idea than anything else that ever happened to him in his entire life—fifteen pages—for to this *one thing*, he felt that he owed all his success and happiness. He concluded by writing: "I hope, therefore, that some of my descendants may follow the example and reap the benefit."

When I first read these words, I turned back eagerly to the page where Franklin began to explain his plan. Over the years, I have re-read those pages dozens of times. It was like a legacy to me!

Well, I thought, if a genius like Benjamin Franklin, one of the wisest and most practical men who ever walked this earth, believed this was the most important thing he ever did, why shouldn't I try it? I suppose if I had ever gone to college, or even high school, I might have felt that I was too smart for such a thing as this. But I had an inferiority complex because I only went to school six years in my whole life. Then when I discovered that Franklin had only *two* years of schooling, and now, 150 years after his death, all the world's greatest universities were showering honors on him, I thought I'd be a fool *not* to try it! Even at that, I kept a secret of what I was doing. I was afraid people would laugh at me.

I followed his plan exactly as he told me how he used it. I just took it and applied it to selling. Of Franklin's thirteen subjects, I chose six, then substituted seven others which I thought would be more helpful to me in my business, subjects in which I was especially weak.

Here is my list, and the order in which I used them:

1. Enthusiasm.
2. Order: self-organization.
3. Think in terms of others' interests.
4. Questions.
5. Key issue.
6. Silence: listen.
7. Sincerity: deserve confidence.
8. Knowledege of my business.
9. Appreciation and praise.
10. Smile: happiness.
11. Remember names and faces.
12. Service and prospecting.
13. Closing the sale: action.

I made up a 3″ x 5″ card, a "pocket reminder," for each one of my subjects, with a brief summary of the principles, similar to the "pocket reminders" you have found throughout this book. The first week, I carried the card on *Enthusiasm* in my pocket. At odd moments during the day, I read these principles. Just for that one week, I determined to double the amount of enthusiasm that I had been putting into my selling, and into my life. The second week, I carried my card on *Order: self-organization*. And so on each week.

After I completed the first thirteen weeks, and started all over again with my first subject—*Enthusiasm*—I knew I was getting a better hold on myself. I began to feel an inward power that I had never known before. Each week, I gained a clearer understanding of my subject. It got down deeper inside of me. My business became more interesting. It became exciting!

At the end of one year, I had completed four courses. I found myself doing things naturally, and unconsciously, that I wouldn't have attempted a year before. Although I fell far short of mastering any of these principles, I found this simple plan a truly magic formula. Without it, I doubt whether I could have maintained my enthusiasm . . . and *I believe if a man can maintain enthusiasm long enough, it will produce anything!*

Here is an astonishing thing to me: I seldom meet anyone who never heard of Franklin's thirteen weeks' plan, but I have never met anyone who has told me he tried it! Yet near the close of his long and amazing life, Benjamin Franklin wrote: "I hope, therefore, that some of my descendants may follow the example, and reap the benefit."

I don't know of anything a sales manager can do for his salesmen that will do so much to assure their success as to make it absolutely compulsory for them to follow this plan.

Remember Franklin was a scientist. This plan is scientific. Reject it, and you reject one of the most practical ideas ever offered you. I know. I know what it did for me. I know it can do the same for anyone who will try it. It's not an easy way. There is no *easy* way. But it is a sure way.

FRANKLIN'S THIRTEEN SUBJECTS
(just as he wrote them down, and the order
in which he used them)

1. *Temperance*—Eat not to dullness; drink
   not to elevation.

2. *Silence*—Speak not but what may benefit
   others or yourself; avoid trifling conversation.

3. *Order*—Let all your things have their
   places; let each part of your business
   have its time.

4. *Resolution*—Resolve to perform what you
   ought; perform without fail what you
   resolve.

5. *Frugality*—Make no expense but to do
   good to others or yourself; i.e., waste
   nothing.

6. *Industry*—Lose no time; be always employ'd in something useful; cut off all unnecessary actions.

7. *Sincerity*—Use no hurtful deceit; think innocently and justly, and, if you speak, speak accordingly.

8. *Justice*—Wrong none by doing injuries, or omitting the benefits that are your duty.

9. *Moderation*—Avoid extremes; forbear resenting injuries so much as you think they deserve.

10. *Cleanliness*—Tolerate no uncleanliness in body, cloaths, or habitation.

11. *Tranquility*—Be not disturbed at trifles, or at accidents common or unavoidable.

12. *Chastity*—Rarely use venery but for health or offspring, never to dulness, weakness, or the injury of your own or another's peace or reputation.

13. *Humility*—Imitate Jesus and Socrates.

35. LET'S YOU AND I HAVE A HEART TO HEART TALK

⇒⇒ ⇐⇐

If I were your own brother, I would say to you what I'm going to say to you now . . . you haven't got much more time!

I don't know how old you are, but let's assume, for example, you are about 35. *It's later than you think.* It won't be long before you are 40. And once you pass 40, time goes so fast. I know. I am now, as I write, sixty-one years old, and I just can't believe it. It makes my head swim when I think how fast time has gone since I was forty.

Now that you have read this book, I think I know how you must feel. Exactly as I would if I were reading it for the first time. You've read so much, by now you may be confused. You don't know what to do about it.

Well there's one of three things you can do about it:

FIRST: Nothing. If you do nothing about it, reading this book has probably been a total waste of your time.

SECOND: You can say: "Well, there are a lot of good ideas here. I'll give them all I've got. I'll do the best I can about it."

If you do that—I prophesy failure.

266

THIRD: You can take the advice of one of the greatest minds this continent has ever produced, Benjamin Franklin. I know exactly what he would say if it were possible for you to sit down alongside of him today and ask his advice. He would tell you to take one thing at a time, and give a week's strict attention to that *one* thing; *leaving all the others to their ordinary chance.*

Whether you are a printer, salesman, banker, or candy push-cart peddler, let's assume that you select thirteen subjects best suited to *you.* By concentrating on one thing at a time, you will get farther with it in one week than you otherwise would in a year. A new confidence will take hold of you. At the end of thirteen weeks, I know you will be surprised with your progress. If your friends, business associates, and your family fail to tell you they have noticed a big change come over you—then *I know,* by the time you repeat the second thirteen weeks, *everybody* will see in you a greatly different person.

I am going to close this book, just as I started it.

When Dale Carnegie invited me to go with him on a lecture tour, the idea seemed fantastic—yet, when I faced those young men of that great organization, the Junior Chamber of Commerce, they inspired me so much that I soon found myself doing what I thought would be impossible—giving three talks every night, five consecutive nights, to the same audience—in thirty cities, from coast to coast.

It seemed even more fantastic for me to write a book. But I started. I have tried to write just as I spoke—the memory of those wonderful faces constantly before me—urging me on. Here it is. I hope you like it.

INDEX

269